THE PROFESSIONS

LIBRARIANSHIP

William R. Maidment

DAVID & CHARLES
NEWTON ABBOT LONDON
NORTH POMFRET (VT) VANCOUVER

ISBN 0 7153 6897 4

Library of Congress Catalog Card Number 75-17

Set in 11 on 13 pt Linotype Baskerville and printed in Great Britain by Latimer Trend & Company Ltd Plymouth
for David & Charles (Holdings) Limited
South Devon House, Newton Abbot Devon

Published in the United States of America
by David & Charles Inc
North Pomfret Vermont 05053 USA

Published in Canada
by Douglas David & Charles Limited
132 Philip Avenue North Vancouver BC

LIBRARIANSHIP

THE PROFESSIONS

Architecture J. M. Richards
Banking Evan Hughes
Medicine Jane Gray
Teaching John Watts

in preparation
Journalism Ion Trewin
The Law John Payne
Radio and Television Stuart Hood

Contents

Introduction

You may have found this book on the shelves of your public library, in which case it would have been chosen by a librarian who has the enviable task of spending many thousands of pounds a year on books. Enviable, but not always easy because there are so many titles to choose from. More than 30,000 are published annually in the United Kingdom alone and about 250,000 titles from earlier years are still in print, to say nothing of the output of other countries. A library is an orderly collection of books and those that are added have to be classified, catalogued and indexed so that the order is maintained and every item can be found when it is wanted. Some of the people who use the library are conversant with the cataloguing and classification systems but others occasionally need guidance or want books not on display. More librarians are needed to help them. Whether he is buying books, cataloguing them, or directly serving readers, the librarian's job is part of a system aimed at offering a reader the book that is right for his purpose.

Few towns are without a public library and it is easy to assume that there are very many librarians to look after all the public and other kinds of libraries, but this is a very small profession. Librarians are not as rare as actuaries, but they are by no means as common as teachers, lawyers, doctors or even clergymen. In the United Kingdom, which has a highly developed library system, the number of chartered librarians has only recently reached 10,000. Other professions are much larger than this: there are nearly 20,000 clergy of the Church of England alone, about twice as many medical practitioners, some 30,000 lawyers and about 400,000 trained teachers.

Librarians are supported in their work by a larger number of library assistants, a small group of administrative staff and, of course, there are attendants, cleaners and other auxiliaries. In public libraries the non-manual staff consists of about 40 per cent chartered librarians and 60 per cent assistants or clerical workers, but the proportion may be quite different in other kinds of library, much depending on the amount of administration which is carried out by the parent institution (university, college etc).

Most of this book is about public libraries because I can write about them from personal experience and because they are the largest employers of librarians. I have tried to reflect librarians' aims and attitudes to their work. Experience in non-public libraries is bound to be somewhat different because these serve specific groups of readers whose needs are more clearly defined, sometimes being limited to one subject treated in greater depth than the general library achieves. The basic techniques of the job are the same and many librarians transfer from one type of library to another, especially in the earlier part of their careers. No one person could have experience of all kinds of library and I can do no more than indicate the differences I have noticed, hoping that my friends in national, university and special libraries will be tolerant of an outsider's view.

CHAPTER ONE

The Library Purpose

King George V once described the public library system as a national university that all may attend and none need ever leave. A notable comment this, just the kind of thing chief librarians like to quote in their annual reports. In the 1930s it was especially pleasing because it stressed education when librarians were uncomfortably aware that a high proportion of library use was recreational. It was quite true that all could attend as everyone in Britain had some kind of library service available but at that time less than 20 per cent of the population made use of it.

Compulsory education provides teachers with a captive audience and some other professional groups are very hard to avoid. By contrast, people can and do live the whole of their lives without seeing the inside of a public library, a museum or an art gallery; librarians always have to remember that the public library is an institution that none need ever attend and all may leave alone. Occasionally one used to meet librarians who wanted nothing better than to be left alone. Recruited when jobs were scarce, their main ambition was to have a safe niche in pensionable employment, preferably in the public services. They saw themselves primarily as officials applying the exact letter of the law and knowing every regulation and by-law by heart. If anyone actually managed to join the library and borrow books this was almost regarded as a defeat for the official.

Fortunately such people are rare today as librarians now have a long training period which includes practical work under supervision. A sense of service tends to develop, whatever the original motives for joining the profession. Obviously, I would prefer to claim that most recruits start with a dedicated desire to encourage people to use libraries and to help them to gain the maximum benefit from books, but I doubt if this is true. I hesitated about revealing my own motives until I came across the following in the *Library Association Record*:

> Like a number of outstanding librarians Eric Clough, the Library Association's President for 1974, came into the profession with, he says, no deep sense of vocation. His career has shown that a sense of vocation can come quickly and in full measure, for it is difficult to imagine a more committed and professional librarian . . .

Good librarians, it seems, are not necessarily born to any precise specification but are made by training. More often, I suspect, they are made partly by training but much more by an infection they catch from working with enthusiasts. Certainly most of my own ideals developed from the good fortune of serving a series of chief librarians I admired, in particular Lionel McColvin, formerly city librarian of Westminster, who influenced ideas about libraries in many parts of the world. From the professional aspect, my initial assets were meagre. I liked books and reading and I expected to enjoy working with the general public but I do not recall analysing my tastes to see if they filled a job specification. I doubt if I even thought about doing any actual work: I just liked spending my time in libraries.

My first experience of a public library came at the age of

seven and it was like entering into a period of gracious living. I was brought up in a small house and I associated school with crowded classrooms and playgrounds. In the library there was room to move and freedom to look through as many books as I wanted before making a final choice. No one demanded to know what I wanted, as they did in shops, and, above all, there was no problem of matching desires with resources: it was all free. Nothing has eradicated these early impressions, indeed when I first secured a job in a library I remember thinking that I was now to be paid for spending my time where I would choose to be anyway. Perhaps I have discovered a new formula for vocational guidance: instead of asking school leavers whether they want to be doctors, barristers, teachers and so on, we might ask them where they want to spend their working lives, in hospitals, law-courts, schools, churches or libraries.

Making a profile of the person who will be happier in a library than elsewhere is not easy because of the variety of libraries which exist to serve different groups of people. A few generalisations, apart from the obvious ones about liking books and being able to work with other people, can be made. Perhaps the most important quality is a sense of order, which is vital in all departments of every library. Books have to be kept in their exact places if they are to be produced when needed and the same applies even more strongly to pamphlets filed in boxes, maps in cabinets and records in racks. An item badly misplaced is effectively lost and if it is found at all it will be by chance rather than skill. An experienced assistant will pick out many misplaced books when tidying the shelves before the library opens but children's books which have been put on the adult shelves or open-shelf volumes wrongly consigned to the reserve store do not draw attention to themselves. A large reference library may have tens of thousands of sheet maps and if a careless librarian files a sheet from a land-use survey in the topographic section it may be cheaper to replace it than to search the whole stock in the hope of retrieving it.

Those who are untidy by temperament are a nuisance in any library and in any department. There is a conflict here, though, because the officious type of librarian I deplored earlier is often meticulous about putting things in the right place as well as in enforcing rules, which is a way of putting people in their places. Achieving a balance between rules and order may be difficult but there are librarians who hate to find a book upside down or mis-shelved but nevertheless feel tolerant about the old lady who has forgotten to bring her library ticket. Tolerance with people and tidiness with things is the happiest combination of qualities for a librarian.

The children's department is the place where tolerance is undoubtedly the first virtue. Impatience at some trivial misdemeanour can drive a child away for good, especially if neither parent nor teacher encourages him to come. Fortunately, children's librarians are often the ones who have made the most deliberate choice of job. Usually they begin with a decision to work with children and then choose librarianship rather than teaching because it means a less formal or disciplined approach. I know of several children's librarians who tried teaching first and then changed after a few years. Others, who started in libraries, have moved closer to the world of education by becoming school librarians. At a more advanced level there are posts in college, polytechnic and university libraries.

Many librarians are more interested in the kind of material they will handle than the sector of society they will serve. Some libraries have a separate department for music and recordings, for instance, and the staff are attracted to the work by their interest in music rather than by a burning desire to serve musicians. If the interest is a strong one, all will be well because the staff find fellow enthusiasts amongst the users which gives an adequate motivation for providing the service needed. Apart from the special departments within public libraries, there are many institutions specialising in particular fields and they often have their own libraries or information services. Whatever subject one thinks of, from agriculture to zoology, there is a library somewhere which specialises in it.

Usually the special-subject librarian finds himself serving a limited group of the population: the medical library obviously existing for doctors, nurses and medical students whilst other institutional libraries are for identifiable groups such as architects, accountants or engineers. The various professions are very different in their use of libraries once they have passed the student stage. Scientists are easy to work with because they have an immediate sympathy with the librarian's systematic approach to information retrieval. Lawyers use libraries a lot, planners quite a bit and architects a little less. Many professional people rely on journals and other sources of information rather than books to keep abreast of modern developments in their subject.

How many librarians start with one of these subjects in mind or with the wish to serve a particular group of people no one can say. Some must drift into librarianship because jobs happen to be available when they leave school or university. However, it is worth noting that in local government, when there are vacancies in several departments, the town clerk and the treasurer find it harder to obtain junior staff and trainees than does the librarian.

I can recall only a few cases of librarians deliberately abandoning the profession for another (excluding, of course, marriage or motherhood) and those that have done so remained connected with books. Some started writing and then, after achieving a success, decided to become full-time authors. John Braine was a branch librarian before *Room at the Top* encouraged him to change and Eric Leyland was well known as a children's author before resigning his post as a borough librarian. Angus Wilson was formerly on the staff of the British Museum library before being appointed a professor of literature as well as becoming a novelist and probably regards himself as a bookman rather than as an ex-librarian.

Occasionally trainees leave without completing their training but the wastage rate is much lower than in teaching and other comparable jobs. Often those who opt out of librarianship were, in the first place, over-persuaded by parents, teachers, or even doctors. Horrified parents whose offspring want to be actresses, models, or artists sometimes think that librarianship will be a lesser evil which might be tolerable because it is (or appears to be) vaguely 'arty'. Career advisers give school leavers excellent information about further education but they cannot possibly know every profession well enough to identify the personality type likely to be happy in it. Recommendations must be treated with caution except when teachers are assessing an applicant's chances in examinations, which they often do with great accuracy. Doctors, especially psychiatrists, imagine that public libraries are hushed places of retreat from the turmoil of the world outside where the disturbed personality will recover its poise. A few encounters with rude or angry readers, of whom every library has its quota, can be disastrous for such patients.

Perhaps the idea of the public library as a peaceful place in which to work is associated with the older buildings, of which there are many, because they have a quite different atmosphere from the replacements which have been appearing in recent years. Almost all libraries are either very old or very modern and there are few central library buildings which can be dated to the period between the wars. The reason for this lies in the origins of the public library movement in the early nineteenth century, to the passing of the first Public Libraries Act in 1850 and, above all, to the benefactions of Andrew Carnegie.

Carnegie began his programme to establish public libraries in 1883, when he offered to provide a building in Dunfermline, which was his birthplace, if the local authority undertook to maintain a library service. The offer was the first of many and led to the rapid spread of libraries. By about 1905, of the municipal libraries which were in use, a few were in buildings put up at the ratepayers' expense and a few were provided by other benefactors, but most owed their existence to Andrew Carnegie's offers. The speed of these developments was impressive but it had one disadvantage: almost all of Britain's libraries were erected within a twenty-year period. All were similar in style, because tastes did not change much during that time, all were new together and all have grown old together. Most of the buildings were still in use in 1960 and many will still be in use in 1980.

There is an endearing aspect about some of the old buildings but they are often quite inadequate to provide the kind of service expected today. However, the staff are more conscious of the disadvantages than are the library users. Readers find old-fashioned tall bookcases a minor nuisance, the top shelf being hard to see, especially for old people, and the bottom one hard to bend down to. The visitors spend only a short time taking books from the shelves but the staff spend some hours every day checking, tidying and replacing books. Everyone is affected by the 'established' feeling of the place, not exactly cathedral-like but retaining a kind of opulence from more spacious days. Sometimes there is a smell from accumulated layers of floor polish and even the lingering fragrance of leather preservative. Woodblock flooring and stained-dark wood panelling add to the general sense of changelessness.

Any spaciousness is, alas, confined to the public departments. Only the staff know of the odd-shaped areas behind the scenes, the awkward steps and cramped rooms, every wall covered with shelves to accommodate reserve stocks. If there is a basement it is overflowing with the accumulated riches of a hundred years of book collecting, every librarian being a reluctant withdrawer until the move to a new building concentrates his mind on this sad task. Odd corners in the basement will be obstructed with peculiar objects accepted by long-gone libraries committees who dared not offend the donors. A life-size sculpture of a local worthy, which once stood in the entrance hall, now obstructs the passage of book trolleys in the book store. Along one wall a glass-doored case is crammed with stuffed birds, relics of the ambition of a committee chairman in the 1920s who always hoped to persuade his colleagues to vote the money to provide a museum of local natural history.

In almost any town which has no local museum one can find strange objects stored in the library, presented and accepted in the hope that one day the deficiency will be remedied. Two of the libraries I have worked in had small armouries. One had a complete set of the various 'marks' of rifle produced by a local small-arms firm, all kept in the cause of history, and the other lovingly retained the weapons of the long-since disbanded Local Defence Volunteers. The oddest discovery was in the chief librarian's office in a suburban building. The office was large because the library committee were accommodated there for their monthly meeting and, at one end, was a large boardroom-type table. This was covered with green baize which almost reached the floor on all four sides. Under the table, completely hidden, was a lead coffin which had been found in a local archaeological dig. Roman coffins are not all that rare but they can be valuable as metal refining was not very advanced in Roman times and the lead contains a goodly trace of silver.

Increasingly, people starting to work in libraries find themselves deprived of these adventures. For a long time extensions of library services were made not by building larger central libraries but by establishing branches. Many of the branch libraries are, therefore, much more modern than the Carnegie buildings. Since about 1960 the experience gained in designing branch libraries has been turned to replacing the eighty- or ninety-year-old central buildings. The change started in London which, within five years, saw new buildings in Kensington, Holborn, Hampstead and Hornsey.

The Holborn library, opened in 1960, was the first to make a real break with the past and to show in material form the kind of developments which had taken place in library services. The borough architect, S. A. G. Cook, was influenced by what he had seen in Scandinavia and managed to translate the exciting designs previously seen only in branch libraries into the scale needed for a much larger building. It is easy to incorporate a friendly atmosphere in a small branch library which gives a personal kind of service and it is not difficult to produce large buildings with many modern facilities for research. The problem is to combine the two techniques so that the ordinary member of the public is not put off by a feeling that the new piece of grand architecture is not really for him. I think the Holborn library achieved this and every subsequent library has been influenced by the change of style. By 1970 there was a long list of new buildings for central libraries and many new university libraries. Most of the librarians involved found it a stimulating experience to work closely with the architects for several years to produce creative designs which would work efficiently.

Much of the new building in the 1960s and 1970s has been due to enthusiasm on the part of local authorities and there would have been even more libraries but for the central government's restrictions on capital expenditure. There are, however, some odd cases where new libraries exist because the old building was in the way of a new road or of some other development dear to the local council. It is said that even the Birmingham central library, the largest public library project of the century in Europe and perhaps in the world, would have been further delayed but for a plan to complete a ring road across the site of the old library. The new building is there and will give benefits for many, many years so perhaps it is wrong to cavil. Few people recall today that Westminster's important library in St Martin's Street, south of Leicester Square, was built against the will of the then city council. A library service, formerly operated from part of the city hall, had been closed and a group of citizens, headed by the vicar of St Martin's-in-the-Field, claimed that the action was illegal. In due course this contention proved to be well founded and the council was ordered by the court to provide a library in the area. The new building, a great improvement on the previous accommodation, was opened in 1925.

Student librarians, as part of their practical training, are taken on tours of new buildings to see the latest techniques in use. After a few experiences they are less willing to work in the worst of the very old buildings, consequently the chief librarian of a new library often finds it is an excellent recruiting agent. Not all librarians, of course, want to work in large libraries. Small branches give a different, more intimate kind of service and the assistant feels less of a cog in a wheel. It is probably a mistake to be *too* much influenced by the surroundings when choosing a job. Some impressive buildings can offer a poor service and the people who work in them have a low morale whilst older buildings carry on a tradition which makes for a happy staff giving a good service in spite of difficulties. Many of the basic duties of a librarian are the same in any library and the kind of people he meets depends on where the library is situated rather than on its age or size.

CHAPTER TWO

A Librarian's Day

Lending libraries usually open at 10 am but the staff have been hard at work for about an hour before that. How hard depends on the day of the week, because the main job is clearing up routine work from the previous day's transactions, re-shelving the books which came in during the closing hours and tidying and checking as much of the stock as can be managed. Monday morning is difficult, as Saturday was almost certainly a busy day which has left its mark. In a small branch library most of the stock was turned over and there is not much order left. The central library with its larger stocks has a bigger proportion undisturbed but there are more shelves to be checked.

This preliminary period is scarcely the library's finest hour but it is a very revealing one. A librarian considering applying for a post would probably learn more about his likely colleagues before the library opens, if only he could see them then, than from any official contacts. The absence of readers removes inhibitions and friends can talk loudly across the room, some even singing at their work. In warm weather assistants shelving books may remove coats and work more comfortably until the friendly attendant gives a general warning that he is about to open the doors to the public. If he is not friendly he takes a wicked delight in being a few seconds early to catch the staff off their guard, just one of the ways his attitude affects the general well-being and happiness of the staff.

At 10 o'clock everything becomes subdued. A few regulars may be waiting at the door, some to look at newspapers and others to browse rather than borrow. Except on Saturdays there is often a slow start and the routine work can continue for a bit. The librarian at the inquiry desk will have spent the first hour allocating work, re-arranging regular duties to cover any absences and making out various returns about the previous day's work. Discipline is achieved with an easy rein but there can be problems at the start of the day. One girl is wearing a trouser suit—wasn't there a staff instruction insisting on dresses or skirts? At a branch library one might take a chance that no one will come round from headquarters this morning but at the central library there is no dodging the issue. Standards of dress and appearance have become quite a problem in recent years because the library staff are part of the local 'civil service' and some ratepayers expect formality. They are sure to be disappointed today but, generally, the librarian will try to set limits to the informality permitted. Standards vary a lot; one chief librarian used to insist that her female staff must not wear sleeveless dresses, a rule which I never quite understood because hemlines and necklines were not specified for either height or depth.

With the initial problems cleared, the librarian on duty starts with book reservations and inquiries from the previous day. Books in stock were dealt with at the time and he probably has untraced items to find in bibliographies. Interruptions from readers during the morning rarely involve any learned queries and a high proportion are demands to know how much longer the inquirer has to wait for a heavily reserved book. Invariably she was told last time that she was next on the list and, as that was a fortnight ago, someone must have been cheating. Readers should never be told just how long they must wait for a book because this is not entirely within the librarian's control, but someone always does make a commitment. No one on the staff admits to getting rid of awkward customers by making optimistic promises but, unless the readers are lying, someone is at fault, for every inquirer is sure it is his or her turn.

I sometimes think public librarians make too much of a fetish of meeting the ephemeral demand for the current best-seller. A very small minority of readers, often only two or three per cent of the total, take up a high proportion of the staff's time and, because they are exceedingly vocal in their demands, persuade the librarian to clear the waiting list by buying more copies than the long-term demand would justify. Few librarians are brave enough to resist the pressure so reserved books are given priority in the cataloguing room and rushed to the library where the fuss is being made. Perhaps we should concentrate more attention and resources on the general stock for the benefit of the other 98 per cent of library users.

THE INQUIRY DESK

The librarian on duty at the inquiry desk has little time for such philosophising. In the smaller library he has to abandon the desk for a time and help at the counter to give the junior staff a break for coffee but, at any time, he will be involved in any problems or arguments which arise. Someone wants to bring a pram into the library because the baby cries if left outside; a tricky decision to have to make because no one wants to be hard-hearted but the rules exclude anything on wheels. If a reader tears a dress on a projection from a pram or falls over a wheeled shopping basket the library authority might have little defence against a claim for damages. Readers tend to walk around lending libraries still glancing at books and the librarian must assume that many of his clients are not looking where they are going. A sensible compromise allows small prams and push-chairs at quiet times but excludes them in the evenings and on Saturdays when the library is crowded and the risks greater.

Then there are the dog-owners who will not be parted from their pets. An Alsatian has been tied up outside by one reader and to put another's tiny dog nearby is an invitation to murder; but the regulations say 'no animals'. It is impossible to yield on this rule, except, of course, for guide dogs for the blind. (Yes, blind people do come to libraries.) The small dog the reader promised to carry is invariably put down for a moment so that his owner can open a book and, if others have also benefited from one's leniency, the resulting disturbance is just too exciting. Dog lovers must live in groups—some libraries I have worked in seemed to be immune from the problem whilst others were rarely without dogs tied up outside. One library had so many that we had complaints about the fouling of footpaths and library entrances, a new difficulty finally solved by putting out a bowl of drinking water at the suggestion of one of the owners, who said dogs will not foul the area where they are offered food or drink. He proved to be right.

The librarian's involvement in these routine affairs at the counters is compensated by the counter staff who quietly help him by dealing with minor inquiries about books. Unless they are very busy they will cope with the regular 'two romances for mum and a murder for dad' type of demand. These are best handled at the counter if only because the best place to look is amongst the recently returned books still awaiting replacement on the shelves. If the messenger brings a list of wanted items it means a trip round the shelves hoping at least one of the titles is in. If there is no list then no one, even in the smallest branch, can hope to remember who has had what before, and the messenger often bounces back again with 'she's read it and it wasn't much good anyway'.

More sophisticated inquiries handled by the librarian include a lot of miscellaneous information which is really the reference department's job but, in a branch without a separate reference library, the simpler items are dealt with on the spot. Addresses of various local buildings are sought by new residents. People with complaints to make want the address of the local member of parliament or a list of ward councillors. Justices of the peace, commissioners for oaths, doctors, estate agents, are all sought by somebody. Eagerness for guidance always means a request for a recommendation which the librarian dare not give, beyond the production of printed lists of doctors, dentists, schools and everything else he is asked for. Some want the citizens' advice bureau or the social security office, whilst middle-class ladies on the warpath want the consumers' association or the weights and measures department. In happier mood, they seek a list of voluntary associations they can offer to join: the Red Cross, Old People's Welfare, friends of hospitals.

Later in the day there are more book inquiries. Readers who usually find their own material by browsing round the shelves occasionally have a specific need and have to be shown how to use a catalogue. Subject locations are so frequently asked for that one scarcely notices: 'Where are the books on radio, France, poetry, geography, witchcraft, Wiltshire, astrology? An endless stream of inquiries comes in random order. 'Who wrote *A Passage to India, The Riddle of the Sands, Three Men in a Boat*?' 'Is de Maupassant under D or M?' 'What is the correct order to read Forester's 'Hornblower' series or Anthony Powell's 'Music of Time' novel sequence?'

Specific subjects tend to follow a seasonal pattern. Holidays are planned earlier and earlier every year so travel and description are sought purposefully in January, to be followed in the spring and summer by guidebooks and maps. Autumn brings requests for background reading for evening class courses or adult-education groups. Indoor hobbies replace the interest in fishing, sailing and sport. Cookery books are at a premium towards Christmas, although they are in fair demand throughout the year. There is no end to the variety. Fathers, whose daughters are about to marry, require books on etiquette and guides to speech-making. Their daughters want books on birth control, housekeeping and, again, cookery. Later on (did the first book let them down?) they come with their prams and want books on baby care. However busy the library, some inquirers feel they must explain why they want something. The father seeking books on etiquette follows the librarian to the shelves explaining that his elder daughter is to be wed and as she is the first in his family he has no experience of giving the bride away. To indicate the urgency of the inquiry he gives the date of the wedding and, if not gently stopped, goes on to say where the reception is to be held, how many guests are invited, the colour of the bride's dress, the number of bridesmaids; in fact, everything that has been on his mind about the subject.

If the library is near a college or senior school there is a rush of students at lunch-time or in the early evening, all of them wanting the same subject if not precisely the same book recommended by a teacher. Sometimes the teachers come themselves and want a booklist prepared for a particular course, thus indirectly warning the library of a future demand which can be prepared for. More often the teachers want material for use in class: illustrations, slides on local history, maps, books on craftwork. Some are referred to the children's library which has more appropriate items in stock.

If there is no college nearby the library has some other specialist demand. The kind of people using any library depends on its location as few users have travelled very far.

By law, some departments are open to anyone who wants to use the library but the legal obligation to lend books is limited to those who reside in the area or who are full-time workers or students. I once worked in a library in central London where only 5 per cent of the members were residents, the rest being office workers from the neighbourhood. Their interests were wide-ranging and they were a demanding public to serve but the main feature of the work was its timing, as they all came in at lunch-time or in the early evening. At midday, the staff, braced for the daily struggle, outnumbered the readers. By 12.15 pm there was a queue to the street and by 12.30 the library was packed with three or four hundred people. For two hours readers came and went but the number in the building remained at that level. At 2 o'clock the queue to enter the library stopped quite suddenly but now there was a queue at the 'out' counter. By 2.15 all was quiet again. This odd pattern of work had the advantage that only a small proportion of the staff was needed in the evenings and Saturday was the quietest day of the week.

Although there are a few part-time branches most library buildings are open sixty or more hours a week whilst the members of the staff each work about thirty-six hours. One of the routine jobs for the librarian in charge of each department is to produce time-sheets which ensure that enough librarians and library assistants are on duty throughout the opening hours. The rota has to take account of the local pattern of use, which, in most residential areas, means that the lending library will be busy in the evenings and all day Saturday. All work behind the scenes is fitted into normal office hours so the share of evenings and Saturdays works out at about two 8 o'clock nights a week and perhaps a duty every other Saturday. Compensating time off duty means having weekdays free, a pattern of life which one soon learns to like.

TYPES OF READER

In a suburban area or a country district the flow of people coming to the library depends on the kind of neighbourhood and, more particularly, on the siting of the library in relation to shops, stations and schools. If it is in a shopping centre many housewives will come in during the day, often changing books for their husbands as well as for themselves. A few local workers and some children arrive at lunch-time and many more in the early evening. Retired people call throughout the day, many spending a lot of time browsing through books and periodicals before borrowing a book for the evening. Family groups come in the early evening or on Saturdays and, from about 7 pm, the library is busy with the returned commuters who did not make use of the city-centre library during the day. Saturday is the peak day, when all the world and his wife may come. Surveys have been made to determine the patterns of library usage by finding which sex, class or age group is most heavily represented but the variations can easily be exaggerated. Whether one joins a library or not depends to some extent on education and, as this has some relationship with social class, it is too easy to generalise and regard the library as mainly a middle-class institution. Certainly in predominantly affluent areas the membership may be around 50 per cent of the population but, even in working-class districts, it is often well over 25 per cent and this understates the usage as many of the men read books borrowed on their wives' tickets.

In almost all libraries there are some scholars, researchers and journalists using the resources to the full; children and the less-educated adults want simple introductions to subjects, workmen want car manuals, travel guides and books on workshop practice; everyone wants to read about hobbies such as gardening, owner-occupiers want to improve or redecorate their homes and the demand for 'do-it-yourself' guidance is insatiable. Fiction is more than half the total of books issued but this does not mean a high proportion of very light escapist literature for there is a steady, continuing demand for the classics in every library. Sometimes this is stimulated by television serials or by stories read on the radio but there are exceptions. Dickens and Jane Austen are always wanted but interest in Galsworthy and Trollope was rekindled by television; for some reason even well-acted versions of Scott and, later, of Henry James did not receive a response from library readers.

In the smaller branches, staff become familiar with the borrowers' tastes and are even told a lot about their private lives. The people who explain why they want a particular book are remembered when there are only a few thousand members and it is not unusual to hear an assistant asking someone if she has heard from her daughter who went to Australia, or another whether her son is enjoying his voluntary service overseas. The librarian's ability to produce information for them before they went builds up a reputation and brings inquiries which are by no means bibliographical. A branch library on a council estate, in particular, serves as an information centre on almost any subject, interpreting notices about rate rebates, rent problems and social services. One branch librarian told me he is the first call when local residents face personal dilemmas such as losing their front-door keys and he is also assumed to know about lost dogs, wounded pigeons found in the street and what to do about ducks which stray from the local park.

Personal service to readers is taken for granted today but it was not originally regarded as essential. In the early days of public libraries readers were not admitted to the main department where they could have handled the books for themselves but had to ask at a counter for their books. The counters were staffed by assistants, whose job was mainly the fetching and carrying, and the librarian had little direct contact with his readers. The basis of librarianship then was serving readers by the choice of books, by supervision of the library and by the production of a catalogue which was essential because readers could not otherwise know what books were available.

When librarians began to admit readers to the lending departments they were creating the first self-service stores, which they called 'open access' libraries. Even before World War I readers were being admitted to the shelves in a few pioneering libraries and by the late 1920s the system was almost universal in England, although a few die-hards resisted the change for a long time. One library in London was still a 'closed access' library until World War II. The change, when it came, meant less emphasis on catalogues because readers could now see for themselves what was immediately available and needed lists only for other material they might want to reserve or look for later. Classification systems to arrange books by subject became essential and thought had to be given to methods of displaying books and of labelling cases and shelves to guide the reader round the library. Open access was opposed by some librarians because they felt they were losing control of the library and because they expected losses due to theft.

For many years the exits and entrances were controlled by wicket gates or turnstiles which could be locked from inside the counter and these devices probably reduced the risk of loss by direct theft. The main losses from lending libraries, however, have usually been incurred when readers move away from an area and take books with them, a drain which has increased with the increasing mobility of the population. Direct loss from the shelves has become greater since the wicket gates were abolished, mostly within the last ten or twenty years, in an attempt to reduce formality to the minimum. Electronic devices which sound an alarm if a book is removed improperly are being installed in some libraries but these and other ways of protecting the stock can be quite expensive.

Straightforward cases of larceny, such as stealing books to sell them, are not very common though of course they do occur. Much more often books disappear because they are taken without the formalities by students who want them for a term or an academic year but then fail to return them. Landladies and the wardens of hostels sometimes discover these treasures in lodgings vacated by students and the books are returned to the library in the end. Librarians used to be more concerned about defacement of books and about damage done by the odd things used as bookmarks. The oft-quoted cases of readers using rashers of bacon for bookmarks are surely apocryphal but all sorts of other things are left in books: highly personal letters, documents of all kinds, banknotes, and even unopened wages packets have been found. Presumably these things happened to be nearest to hand at a moment of interruption in reading. Open access has probably had very little net effect on either book losses or on the care of books in other ways. It has made it possible for readers to become more discriminating because they can read the publicity matter on the dust jacket of a book, look at the preface and even read a few pages before deciding whether to borrow it.

BOOK SELECTION AND STOCK

The other important effect of open access is that librarians can help readers in the choice of books, explain the arrangement of the library and elucidate the mysteries of the catalogue. Direct face to face meetings with library users is an essential part of a librarian's assessment of his bookstock because no analysis of the records of books borrowed can give a clear picture of the real issue for the reader—what is there on the shelves at this moment? The trouble with running a lending library is that it exists to lend books. If it is successful, the best of the stock ought to be in the readers' homes, but it will soon cease to be successful if what is left on the shelves does not please. Newly published books are usually chosen at headquarters to provide a wide range of titles for the whole library system but the librarian in charge of a department has some say in what is sent to his particular branch. He also has full responsibility for stock maintenance, which means ordering extra copies, withdrawing unwanted duplicates and making decisions about replacements, rebinding and transfers to reserve. No training in techniques of book selection can equal the comments of readers complaining about inadequacies of the stock or the embarrassment of the librarian who takes a reader to the shelf for a specified subject and finds nothing adequate. To know that there is a local demand for books on tropical fish is a useful piece of knowledge and, if there are a dozen titles in the catalogue with several copies of each on loan, then something worthwhile is being achieved. Self-satisfaction is soon deflated if one more reader asks for the subject and nothing is available. He may be persuaded to reserve something but this is a second best to immediate service. He is unlikely to be interested in explanations about the sudden demand or the number of titles in stock. He really does not want a request card or an explanation. He wants a book.

The qualified staff in a lending library spend about half their time directly dealing with readers and divide the remaining hours between administration, staff organisation, reservations and stock control. There is never enough time to do all that one would like but somehow a few hours must be spent at the shelves every week, noting deficiencies in particular subjects or authors, removing superseded editions and so on. Worn out or damaged books should be spotted by the counter staff and a trolley full will be taken to the workroom every day for the librarian to check. Inquiry desk experience and up-to-date knowledge of the shelf stock are needed to make sensible decisions about whether to discard, relegate to reserve or keep on open shelves by rebinding or replacing. Is there a cheap edition available? Has there been a paperback edition which might reduce library demand?

All the decisions need further action. Books for the binder have to be listed, counted and checked before despatch and every month there are cartons of rebound books to check. Withdrawn items are noted so that catalogues and shelf records can be adjusted. Replacements have to be ordered. Usually a specified sum will be allocated to each lending department from the annual budget and the librarian's decisions have to be tailored to the resources. This discipline is good training for the more senior posts which may come later on, usually involving a move from controlling a department to allocating resources from the much-maligned central administration.

Branches rely heavily on the central library for their more advanced inquiries and they are in daily contact for help with inter-library lending of books, solving reference queries and preparing booklists. A constant frustration is the reliance which has to be placed on the central library for staff appointments and transfers and for temporary reliefs to cover sickness and holidays. Branch librarians always complain about interminable delays in replacing broken windows, re-washering taps and all the trivia of maintaining a public building; 'the central' is the scapegoat for most things. Books never come soon enough after publication, the chief librarian never comes often enough to see the problems for himself . . . one could go on indefinitely but, in spite of it all, the branch librarian has one of the best jobs in the profession. He controls a unit small enough for him to oversee the whole service but still an independent command in very many respects.

STAFF MEETINGS

Common problems are frequently aired at meetings of branch librarians under the chairmanship of the chief librarian. In many library systems all heads of lending departments attend once a week at the central library to consider the new books and, once a month, the visit is extended to take in a regular meeting. It starts with a few formal items and instructions by the chief librarian and proceeds to any problems the branch librarians themselves want to raise. A typical meeting included the following items:

Booklists—the chief librarian asked how the public had responded to a new series of lists of books on topical subjects. Some branch librarians said the demand was for lists of recent books on all subjects rather than for retrospective lists. After discussion it was decided to continue the subject lists for a time but to improve their appearance. The chief asked for volunteers to prepare lists on their pet topics.

Squatters—the central lending librarian asked whether a man who admitted to being a squatter in an empty house could be allowed to join the lending library. There was a spate of similar problems raised by others. If a squatter is not a resident what about people staying for a short time in a hotel? The chief gave interim guidance but undertook to get a legal opinion and then consult the committee.

Redecorations—a question was raised about the difficulty of continuing 'business as usual' whilst a branch library was being repaired or redecorated. After discussion there was almost unanimous support for the chief's policy of keeping libraries open whenever possible.

Large print books—one branch librarian said that the policy of having a standing order for a series of books for the partially sighted was wrong. His branch had more books than they could display. Immediately others claimed they never had enough of these volumes and would accept any surpluses. The stock editor was invited to survey the whole question in consultation with the branch librarians.

Lots of more trivial items arise at these meetings and often they can be dealt with simply by discussion, the chief librarian entering into it but not having to issue any instructions. A difficulty in one place has frequently been experienced and successfully coped with elsewhere. Minor irritations which are unavoidable in a public service must sometimes be endured rather than cured but there is some comfort in discovering that most of one's colleagues have equally cussed readers. A lurid account of the oddities of people will always be capped by someone else's account and a sense of humour puts the whole thing into perspective.

Looking back on my own years in lending libraries I find that the minor irritations of readers or the central administration are not the things that stand out. The satisfaction of doing an interesting job and having a good deal of freedom of action is clear and the only real regret I remember was the lack of time for systematic control of the bookstock. If readers are waiting for attention they have priority over any 'behind the scenes' duties; if the chief librarian calls a meeting one has to drop everything and attend. Weekly cash returns must be made to balance and be submitted on time if one is to stay out of prison; broken windows and leaking radiators must be reported at once. Stock editing receives any time that is left and one always feels it should have come first.

WORK WITH CHILDREN

A small girl waited patiently at the counter in the children's library until the librarian had time to talk to her. Having finally gained the necessary attention she asked for books on the stars. She pored over everything the librarian could offer from the small astronomy section, rejecting books one by one, refusing help. Finally at the end of fifteen frustrating minutes the librarian asked, 'Can you tell me EXACTLY what you are looking for?' After hesitating for a few more seconds the girl replied, 'Well, I want to find out if I am a LEPRECHAUN.'

No doubt the child learnt a lot from the simple inquiry and, as it arose from a query she herself raised, there is a good chance that the distinction between astrology and astronomy and a brief glance at folklore might stay in her mind. She was lucky to be using a library which had a librarian specifically to help children. The practice is, alas, not universal. In the previous chapter I mentioned how I first joined my local library when I was seven years old and how much I enjoyed it. I did not know until many years later that there were books which I would have enjoyed as a child if I had been guided to them. This loss is something which cannot be remedied later as the impact of a book on the child for whom it is written may be enormous but, if it is read much later in life, the quality can be appreciated intellectually but the magic no longer works.

Perhaps a lingering sense of grievance makes me feel particularly strongly about the neglect of children's work which was so long a feature of public libraries and is, even now, not fully remedied. Any librarian who wants to work with children has to choose the place of work very carefully. There are very many one-room branch libraries which have a section for children but no one is specially appointed to look after their interests. Sometimes the books are well chosen and adequate in number because there is a head of children's work at the central library who chooses the stock and organises the school library service, but this is offering only half a loaf if there is no one specially trained to help the children in the library. The one-room branch has many handicaps for a children's librarian, even if there is one, as story hours and other activities are difficult to arrange.

With sorrow I have to admit that the existence of a separate room for children is no guarantee that the library is a good one to work in if one wishes to specialise in helping children. I have known many libraries with a large room set aside for children which was normally completely dead until 4 pm when it was opened for children for some three hours. During the day the librarian in charge of the building would send a junior assistant into the children's department to tidy the bookshelves and, perhaps, to write any necessary overdue book notices. In the larger places a staff roster showed that someone, usually the least experienced assistant, was detailed to open the children's room at 4 pm. In smaller libraries the branch librarian might come to the main counter at a few minutes before zero hour and, in default of a volunteer, pick someone who had not suffered this particular penance lately.

The contrast with the more progressive libraries could not be more striking. In the last few years more and more libraries have at least a few children's librarians so that, apart from the work at headquarters, real contact can be made on the ground. A few libraries, though still not enough, have a trained librarian for every children's room they have. It is incredible that one should have to mention this as if it were an achievement—any other arrangement is like having a headmistress for a school but no teachers in the classrooms. Where the work is being done properly the children's library has few dead periods. School classes are brought to the library by their teachers for instruction in the use of books and libraries and, later on, they come for work on projects and essays.

A busy library may have ten or more class visits a week to fit in, the age range covering from about four to five years old up to nine or ten years old. Children above this range sometimes come for project work but, usually, this is by special arrangement and not a regular weekly or fortnightly visit. The pattern of activity varies with the age group. First the librarian is busy taking in all the returned books and then there is a period of instruction or help in finding essay or project material. A general dash round follows as everyone tries to find a book to take out but, before they leave, the children expect a story. Finally there is a mad rush to check out all the books as the class must be back at school for the next period.

Why story hours remain so popular in these sophisticated days of television and other mechanical marvels is hard to explain. The facts are clear; every class demands its story. Mothers always turn up with their smallest for the weekly under-fives story session and no alternative entertainment will do. Some children's librarians encourage children to come by amusing them with their own talents of origami or puppet making but these are taken as extras; the story time is still essential. For the smallest, a picture book is usually the basis of a tale whilst the older ones love traditional stories or (yes, even today), fairy stories. Libraries that are more generously staffed are beginning to go out into the streets to attract their child readers or, at any rate, into the parks and squares. The London Borough of Lambeth, in particular, has a lively head of children's services who, missing the class visits during the school holidays, goes out to where the children are likely to be found.

I have sometimes quietly trespassed on a story hour and am always impressed at the attention given to the story-teller or reader. Even in 'tough' districts there is rarely any trouble: they do listen. The very small ones usually sit on cushions, small stools or even on the carpet. As the plot thickens the group seems to get nearer and nearer the librarian, anxious not to miss a word.

Class visits and story hours are merely ways of introducing children to libraries in groups so that the shy individuals are not left out. Everyone in the group is persuaded to join the library and, armed with the membership card, would have to be very timid indeed to be afraid to go into the now familiar library to read and borrow books. The individual calls are spread over several hours in the evenings and most of the day on Saturdays. If the library is near a school there can be a rush period soon after 4 o'clock but this soon tails off to a more casual flow of arrivals. Many libraries open their children's rooms all day during school holidays. These are the most rewarding times for the children's librarian as the pressure is less and the children ask for what they want themselves, following their own ideas without the constraints of school demands.

Of course, every good teacher tries to build on a child's own interests but a syllabus must exercise constraints. The librarian does not need to enliven specified subjects but simply develops any interests which are expressed. If Tommy wants a book on aeroplanes then a book on aeroplanes will be found for him. If he comes back and says he liked it there may be opportunities to discover whether his enthusiasm is for travel, for engines or the techniques of flight. The basic interest can then be followed up. It may be that the one book tells him all he wants to know on the subject at this stage and his next request is for a book on tadpoles; the choice is his.

Perhaps I should have written that the choice ought to be his or is usually his. Sometimes, especially in 'better class' areas, one finds parents over-anxious about a child's reading and pressing their own childhood's enthusiasms instead of allowing complete freedom. Of course there are immense advantages in a home which contains books and in having parents who like reading but, for the librarian, there are more real satisfactions in opening the eyes of a grubby urchin to what books have for him than there are in supplying Arthur Ransome or A. A. Milne to the whim of a parent. At the other end of the spectrum there are parents who seem to have the minimum interest in their children; every children's librarian in a large town knows of 'latch-key' children who haunt the library during school holidays because both parents are at work. The librarian, if she is not careful, becomes a substitute mother.

OTHER ACTIVITIES

For all children useful activities can be arranged during the holidays. In place of class visits one can offer films, puppet shows and talks. Recently we have found that sets of draughts and chessmen in libraries are being well used by children but one has to keep in mind that the basic purpose of the library is to supply books and other reading material. Generally the other activities do not rival the book as the visitor, once in the library, also glances at magazines or books and almost always takes something home, perhaps to read in bed. The main trouble about attracting lots of children in the holidays is that they stay longer than they could on schooldays and, if they get bored, can get up to mischief. Disciplinary problems are usually much less than a teacher faces daily but sometimes a child has to be ejected as a troublemaker. Suspending a ticket for a week can be an effective punishment but one hates to do it in case the boy or girl concerned abandons the library altogether. This is the ultimate failure. I also dislike writing to headmasters asking them to intervene on a disciplinary matter or to secure the return of overdue books. Although school classes are welcome, the library must be kept apart as something distinct from school, otherwise the child leaves the library behind when he leaves school.

I am sure that children should enter a library by the same door as adults and, preferably, return their books to the same counter. They then regard libraries as rather like shops, places which are 'neutral', used by all age groups and classes of people. I doubt whether children really mature earlier today than they used to but the important thing is that they regard themselves as grown up. Few girls past the age of twelve would be seen going through a door marked 'Children's Library' and, if we want them to come, we must adjust our systems to them. For the same reason I dislike regulations which specify the age at which a child may transfer to the adult library—why not leave it to the child to use whichever he finds most acceptable?

My real 'hate' in librarianship is the 'intermediate' or 'teenage' department. I suffered from one of these in my youth as our local library boasted of pioneering the idea of a department which bridged the gap between children and adults. One belonged to the children's department until the age of fourteen and then transferred to the intermediate library until seventeen. The idea was to prevent the loss of membership which often occurred when children left school but, in practice, it merely made two chances of lost readers instead of one. At that time compulsory education ended at the age of fourteen and all those who left school at that age to go to work also left the library. As working adults they had no intention of entering anything less than the adult library. This left mostly the grammar school and girls' high school to provide members for the intermediate library. It was a very useful trysting place and I enjoyed going there but not, alas, for books. Lambeth, which has done so much for youth libraries, tried to solve this by having a kind of youth annexe opening off the adult library in a recent building. Each time I have seen it the occupants were all old age pensioners who welcomed the extra seating provided. I was delighted to read in a recent survey that Lincoln Central Library, which included a specially designed library for adolescents, had a smaller percentage of users between the ages of 15 and 19 than two other libraries checked at the same time. I could have told them so. No doubt anyone reading this will have realised that, however neutral librarians may be on book selection, they can be opinionated on other things. Nevertheless, if asked to advise I would always say never work in a 'youth' department. Prejudice, bias, unfortunate experience . . . whatever you like, but the advice is sound.

Finally, before leaving children and young people I should add that the job has one thing in common with that of a branch librarian. The work is satisfying, creative and worthwhile. It means, in a good library, a busy life. But . . . there is always the frustration amid all the activities of not having enough time for the books. Fortunately, there are fewer books produced for children and the total a child can read in a few short years can be counted in hundreds rather than thousands. Nevertheless, the children's librarian must read children's books as well as their reviews and must balance a tight budget between very expensive picture books, which soon become well worn by the youngest children, the standard children's classics and the latest wonder. The efforts are amply rewarded by the sight of a child completely absorbed in a book, really 'lost to this world', and by the noisier experience of greeting the eager rush of children into the library after school. Opinions are expressed without pretence, enthusiasm is uninhibited. The only time I can remember having to curb enthusiasm was when I found a girl trying to stuff a book behind a radiator. It appeared that she had found two books she had sought for some time and, having only one ticket with her, intended to take one book and collect the other next time. This had to be rebuked, of course, and a librarian should try to inculcate respect for books, but one does like a keen reader.

CHAPTER THREE

Information and Service

All librarians spend part of their time giving information. Some of the inquiries mentioned in the previous chapter were for facts rather than for named books and, in most cases, they could easily be answered in the lending library or children's department. Simplicity can be deceptive on occasion. I recall a request for information about the weight of a seagull, the inquirer having the impression that he had read somewhere that seagulls are amazingly light for their size. He had been referred to the reference library after searching every likely book on the shelves of the lending department. The reference stock did not solve the problem; we could tell him everything on species, sizes and shapes, colour, feeding habits and breeding preferences but could find no reference to weight. It was more than likely that if the fact had appeared in print a specialist library would have indexed it and so it proved. A telephone call produced the answer and also the reference which was to the correspondence columns of a periodical.

We never knew why the information was wanted but it was probably no more important than a matter of settling an argument with a friend. Another ornithological inquiry, which could not be solved by telephone, occurred at a larger reference library in London. A dear old lady came in and asked to see a coloured picture of a peacock's tail fully open. She made no secret of her reason for making the request but said it was in connection with her hobby of embroidery. She stood in the centre of a department with tens of thousands of books and addressed her inquiry to one of half-a-dozen learned librarians. They checked the zoology section and then the travel section and they looked through the files of geographical and natural history magazines without coming across what was wanted. She was on the point of departure when someone thought of trying the children's library and triumphantly returned with a volume of a children's encyclopaedia.

Neither of these experiences could be regarded as a failure as the required item was finally produced. Generally, the reference librarians can supply the answer to inquiries from their own stock. This usually includes the standard books on most subjects, general encyclopaedias and dictionaries, language dictionaries, gazetteers and so on. These are supplemented by an ever-growing mass of pamphlets, leaflets, maps and a quick-reference collection of directories, time-tables and guides. Much of the information given out by the branch librarians is supplied by the central reference library which keeps up to date all the changing facts about addresses, rent rebates, taxation, licensing and so on. There are even books which have to be kept up to date with amendment sheets sent by the publishers: *Export Data Directory*, *Customs and Excise Tariff*, *International Register of Civil Aircraft*. Fortunately, except in the largest libraries, reference librarians have less of the administrative chores of lending librarians but a lot of time is needed for the basic organising of up-to-date information.

Much of the filing and indexing is done at the reference library counter by assistants whose primary duty is to be available to answer inquiries. This can be a little difficult because some readers actually apologise for interrupting and, I suppose, some assistants even let their expressions show that a task they hoped to finish that day was more important to them. The arrival of readers is so erratic that few libraries could afford to keep staff completely idle at the desk and the background work has to be done. However, the whole exercise is pointless unless inquiries are welcomed and most reference staff do want to help. In the larger departments each assistant has a particular area of interest. One may have special responsibility for government publications, another for periodicals. Usually looking after periodicals includes sorting out sets for binding up in volumes. Current numbers have to be checked in daily, which means an even flow for newspapers but an uneven daily rate for magazines which mostly arrive on Fridays and Saturdays. A large library may have over a hundred titles to check on Friday morning and quite a number will be filed permanently, which means eventually making up the individual volumes, obtaining indexes and sending the completed unit to the binder.

The back files are indispensable tools in reference work. Ideas and newly discovered facts are reported in journals and proceedings of learned societies long before they appear in books and inquirers often produce their long lists of references to consult. Journalists and authors make great use of the files of national newspapers, especially when they are writing about centenaries, coronations or other events which would have made the headlines or been featured in illustrated magazines. Most large libraries now have their files of *The Times* available in the department on microfilm and local newspapers can often be produced in this form as well.

Authors use references quite regularly to ensure that the facts are accurate if they are writing non-fiction and that they make no howlers if they are writing novels. When were lighthouses first built? Was there a lifeboat service before then?

How did a Spanish soldier salute an officer in the eighteenth century? How many people would there be in the crew of an ocean-going ship in Tudor times? When was iodine first used to dress wounds? Is it possible to trace an authentic record of the names of convicts transported to Australia? All these are genuine examples of the questions asked in a single library.

Students with specific tasks outside a fixed syllabus can cause a lot of work. Senior pupils at schools take on projects for completion during the summer vacation and many of them ask for so much aid that one wonders who is doing the work. Worst of all are the students who do not call but write, usually giving a very wide field of reference. 'Please send me everything you have about Hampstead Heath as I am doing a project on commons.' To write back in order to narrow the area of search would result in endless correspondence and one can only say 'come to the library'. Advanced students are more likely to define their needs. Helping with the literature for a thesis can be justified, provided the librarian is not expected to do the searching, but most student work takes a lot of time and the librarian can usually do no more than provide the books.

Other library users can look after themselves without help from the staff. Quite often, students like to work in libraries because the atmosphere is more conducive to study than their own homes or bed-sitters and the ready availability of standard texts, dictionaries and photocopying equipment is a help. Whether students attend in any numbers depends on the nearness of colleges and schools so, once again, I have to add that the clientele of all departments depends enormously on the location of the library.

With all the careful indexing and organisation of knowledge there should be no element of luck in reference work, but there is. No book can contain all there is to say on any subject and even general encyclopaedias in numerous volumes omit much of human knowledge. A small, one-volume handbook may have just the item being sought and, though long experience in handling books helps a lot, there is still an element of chance. I once had the odd experience of being asked the same, fairly obscure question twice in fifteen minutes. Apparently there were three cottages not far from the library which were on land owned by the Crown. The occupants held them under a special kind of tenure different from the usual freehold or leasehold. A change in the law had some importance to their rights and all received a notice about it. On a Saturday afternoon one of them came to the library to check the meaning of a legal term which was crucial to the point of the notice. I found it in a general work—I think it was Stone's *Justices Manual.* Soon after the inquirer had left, another man, without giving the same explanation, came to the desk and asked for the definition. Without looking up I said, 'There is a large blue book on the table over there; your definition is on page 1192 starting about half-way down.' He said 'Thanks very much' and started walking across the room. After taking a few paces he glanced round suspiciously, obviously suspecting a leg-pull. He then hurried on, found the place, and looked at me with awe. I hope he did not chat to his neighbour—he may still think librarians know the contents of every book in detail.

These straightforward questions by local people needing help in their everyday affairs are always welcomed by reference library staff, although one must be careful with legal and medical queries which are aimed at checking on professional advice. Lots of people are convinced they could conduct their own legal affairs (and even their own cases in court) better than any lawyer and all they need is a chance to read the subject up. Medical competence is less often questioned but patients suspect the doctor 'is keeping something from them' because their interesting symptoms, which they are willing to divulge to the librarian in intimate detail, must mean a disease more serious than the triviality mentioned by the doctor.

Another type of inquiry which needs great caution is one asking help in valuing a prized possession. It is not unreasonable to ask a librarian a question about a book believed to be a first edition but, if he is wise, he will let the reader check the detailed descriptions given in bibliographies and try to avoid any firm identification. Pricing, assuming the book really is fairly rare, is simply a matter of what an antiquarian bookseller will pay or what can be got at auction. One can produce records of what books have fetched at auction for some years back and, with patience, one can find recent sales recorded in the national newspapers but it would be unwise to put too much faith in such figures. The exact condition of a book, the fact that another copy has changed hands recently, all sorts of things can affect the price.

Stamp collectors do their own searching in Stanley Gibbons' stamp catalogues but sometimes want to borrow a magnifying glass and occasionally want a sympathetic listener if something seems to be exceptionally rare. The magnifying glass is also used for precise checking of hallmarks on precious trinkets and is sometimes borrowed by older people trying to read the small print of regulations, time-tables and other condensed guides. These are fairly routine matters in most libraries and even the stamp collector who spreads his collection over an entire table and pores over items for hours on end is making a reasonable use of the library. I am not quite sure what I ought to have done about the man who arrived with several plastic bags containing the innards of a bicycle three-speed gear; he wanted to reassemble it and there were no books in the lending library giving the clear illustrations he wanted. Another assistant had refused even a short loan of the one reference book which could help.

Today one can solve this kind of difficulty by photocopying, as even quite small libraries now have the equipment for this, but it is necessary to know the legal position under the Copyright Act which gives libraries certain privileges.

Another area where care is needed is giving precise answers as if they were facts rather than stating 'according to . . .' and adding what the book says. This is especially important if an inquiry is made by letter, and on some matters one has to add that the authorities differ. Occasionally the reason for the different answers can be discovered but one may have to consult an authority directly. A simple illustration of how even books which are household names can differ was quoted in a library journal a few years ago. The writer had been asked the height of Nelson's column in Trafalgar Square and, for some reason, compared the answer given in a well-known guide book with the entry in an encyclopaedia. The two answers were so different that he continued checking and found that seven highly respected works gave answers varying from 145 to 185 feet. There is no simple explanation for the small differences between some authorities (two said 184 feet and two said 185 feet) but the wide gap is easily explained. Simple though the question appears, it is imprecise. The complete monument consists of a statue of Lord Nelson standing on a column, which is supported on a plinth. Most English people will think of the complete unit as Nelson's column but the question could refer to the column and statue, excluding the plinth, or even to the column alone.

It may be thought that the exact height of Nelson's column is not likely to be very important to a casual inquirer but the librarian has no right to ask why the information is being sought. Perhaps a large prize for a general knowledge competition is in dispute! Enthusiasts for competitions, quizzes and crosswords rarely take up much staff time since they become conversant with their likely sources and commonly do their own research. There have been exceptions, however. Some years ago, a national newspaper ran a publicity campaign which involved publishing six questions every day and offering very large prizes for competitors with the largest cumulative total of correct answers. This attracted a number of entries from those who were regular readers of the newspaper but not normally concerned with competitions. One London reference library was so inundated with callers asking for help with the questions that the ordinary work of the library was seriously interrupted. The senior staff conferred and it was decided to solve the problem by putting the answers to the day's questions on a notice-board first thing every morning. Some of the junior staff thought this rather unsporting but were, at the same time, impressed by the calm assumption that the department could be so sure of producing all the answers. There is no record that any member of the staff was tempted to enter for the competition.

Most librarians welcome the general information inquiries from local citizens as a relief from the heavy use of reference libraries by students. Apart from personal interests many libraries have to provide in greater depth for subjects relevant to local industries or commercial activities. Some towns have organised a kind of information consortium by providing links between the public reference library, the libraries of colleges and institutes and those of industrial firms. The ever-increasing need for commercial information, especially in connection with the export trade, has led to the division of some reference libraries into two departments, one being the main general reference library with a bias towards the humanities and the other dealing with commerce, law and related subjects. A few of the very largest libraries have subdivided into a number of subject departments. Librarians obviously have to decide whether they prefer the very general nature of the smaller reference library or want to start to specialise.

THE COMMERCIAL LIBRARY

The tempo of the work in a commercial library is quite different from that experienced in even a busy general library. For one thing there are usually far more quick reference inquiries made by telephone. These are for such things as telephone numbers or addresses anywhere in the world, for the manufacturers of proprietary materials, for makers of specified products, or for any of the hundred and one items that can crop up in a commercial office during the course of the day. There is also a steady stream of callers who want information fairly quickly although, unlike the telephone callers, they can read it for themselves once they are helped to find the right book, pamphlet or document. Government publications are heavily used for information about all kinds of regulations and procedures and, together with the reports of international organisations, they provide a valuable source of statistical data. Although I mentioned earlier that one assistant may have special responsibility for the acquisition and checking of such publications it is impossible to refer all the inquiries to him. Everyone working in the department needs to know the way parliamentary papers are issued and arranged by the library and how far reports are placed with the issuing department of state. As far as possible the librarian who is asked for some information by a member of the public produces it himself.

Even in this department there is a special welcome for the individual, such as the local shopkeeper, who cannot afford a legal department or accountant to look after relevant regulations, yet needs to know the answer to such questions as: How much meat must there be in a pork sausage? Does the law require ice-cream to have any specified amount of milk products in it? What is the latest order relating to opening hours of shops? What is the law about stocking fireworks in a shop? Sometimes a town's chamber of commerce will issue a magazine with general information for its members and much of this is gathered from material at the local commercial library. Longer inquiries, requiring a certain amount of research, are made by journalists, especially those working for trade magazines, by authors of books on management or other business subjects, by economists and by teachers of commercial subjects.

THE HUMANITIES DEPARTMENT

The general or humanities library has quite a different atmosphere. Almost all the inquiries related in the earlier part of this chapter were made in general reference departments dealing with a quite unpredictable range of subjects. Where a commercial department exists the other library tends to receive more inquiries involving prolonged research. Larger libraries provide separate study carrels so that once the material has been assembled it can be kept together until the reader has completed his task. A writer, for instance, may need to take notes from a large number of sources to provide background material for a historical novel or the social historian may want to browse through long runs of newspapers and other periodicals covering the time of his study. The librarian may not be required to do more than collect listed material for such library users but he often has to give guidance on sources and even on the use of catalogues and indexes. The simpler factual questions do arise: the dates of birth or death of poets, artists or musicians. Slightly longer biographical answers may be solved by offering the reader a biography of the person named. Tracing quotations is a fairly frequent exercise which is easy, whilst finding the artist who painted a named picture can be difficult. The inquirer who insisted on humming a few bars of a tune he wanted to identify (it really did happen) was hastily directed to the music library.

Although these general questions can be raised by almost anyone there is, among librarians, some regret that reference libraries are not used enough by working-class people for information on the ordinary affairs of life. Branch libraries, as I mentioned in a previous chapter, are used in this way but librarians still have a lot to do if reference libraries are to be as 'neutral' or classless as lending libraries. In the world of information there are big gaps between those whose education or way of life leads them to use reference libraries, read 'quality' newspapers, belong to consumer associations, or read any official handouts relevant to their affairs and the other part of the population which still relies heavily on oral communication with its distortions, inaccuracies and half truths. Television and radio have to some extent replaced the printed word in giving facts but their announcements are ephemeral in the sense that one cannot turn back the pages to correct or confirm something partly recalled.

When people from the less-privileged groups can be persuaded to use a reference library their first attempt is often on a simple practical query, eg at what age is one allowed to drive a heavy goods vehicle? If they receive a friendly welcome they may drop in from time to time with queries about hobbies, games and 'do it yourself' activities. These are the people who produce those devastatingly simple questions which, from the librarian's point of view, are the wrong way round. It is easy to find out the definition of a philatelist or of a numismatist but not so easy to discover the word for a collector of match-box labels or of cigarette cards. However important or trivial the question, it is, in my own experience, perfectly welcome to librarians who tend to feel that the ordinary man in the street gets too little from his reference library which is full of students, many of whom ought to be served by university or college libraries.

One category of user is less welcome in most libraries, although the librarians have no right to refuse help: he is the debt collector or inquiry agent for hire purchase finance firms. He is a regular caller at many reference libraries and spends hours poring over electoral registers checking names and addresses. At one time much of the checking was done by telephone but, as living on credit became respectable or, at any rate, much more general, the calls became longer and longer and some reference libraries found this tedious task took up too much time. Even more important was the continued use of a telephone line which might be more urgently needed by someone else. It might have been embarrassing for one library to adopt a cavalier attitude but, in London, it was possible to reach general agreement amongst the boroughs and all ceased to deal with these inquiries by telephone.

Other wasters of time who cannot easily be disposed of are the odd characters with obsessions of one kind or another. I remember a man who appeared perfectly rational when he came in and asked for biographical information about Lewis Carroll. While he was being taken to the appropriate section of the library he said that he was proud of his direct descent from the writer. However, he appeared unaware that Lewis Carroll was a pseudonym. He was not put off by the discovery that Charles L. Dodgson (Carroll's real name) was a bachelor. Perhaps the descent was from a brother or sister, he said, and proceeded to do some more searching. This man came into the library once or twice a week for several months carrying out an ever-widening and ever more unlikely search. Finally he arrived one morning and came to the inquiry desk. I said that I could not think of anything about Lewis Carroll which he had not had already. 'Lewis Carroll?' he said, as if he had never heard of him, 'I want some books about management.' I found him something and, before I could escape he said: 'I hope it is an advanced work. I have applied for an important job, one that is suitable only for a public school man or a "Varsity man".' I tried to look impressed. 'I am,' he said and paused, 'a PUBLIC SCHOOL MAN.' I said, placatingly, that one could see that. 'And,' he added with even more emphasis, 'a "VARSITY MAN".' He then departed and never returned.

One could fill several books with tales of the eccentrics who have appeared in reference libraries, especially in the central libraries of big cities. Most of them cause no trouble but harmlessly pursue their useless researches. One tries not to be too sure that they are irrational—after all, the first scholar who went into a library to try to prove that Shakespeare's plays were written by Francis Bacon was probably regarded as an eccentric by the librarian. Judging by the vituperation which appears in scholarly journals one might think that, in any literary controversy, the opposing sides each regard themselves as sane and the others as either mad or wilfully obtuse. However, the average eccentric in a public reference library is not of this calibre. Very occasionally one of them causes some kind of disturbance which prevents others using the library in peace and then one has to take action. They mostly go quietly or with only muttered objections. One noisy character I remember had been a regular caller at a library, without causing more than mild amusement, and had been nicknamed 'Old Beany Eye'. (I cannot remember anything about him to justify the name but the staff commonly find names for these people.) Old Beany Eye was normally quiet but one day he stood up in the reference library and started declaiming. He was escorted out by an attendant but remained on the steps of the library, his hands cupped to his mouth like a megaphone and still shouting. I could see him from my office window and, thinking we really had no choice but to telephone the police, I opened the window to hear what it was all about. He was shouting: 'This is the best library in London and I don't care who knows it.' I shut the window and left him to leave when he wished.

The main gathering place of eccentrics is the newspaper and magazine room, where it still exists. Most modern libraries either divide the periodicals between the reference library proper (for technical journals) and the lending department (for popular ones) or else have an annexe to the reference library which has periodicals on display. The early Carnegie libraries had a newspaper room as one of the major features and it was often near the main entrance. Since the war a lot of these rooms have been incorporated into expanded lending libraries but there are still some in existence. An important feature was the newspaper 'slope' which adorned the walls so that readers had to stand to read and thus would not take longer than was necessary. The tables in the centre were for weekly and monthly periodicals and one could sit to enjoy them, although hard chairs were usually the order of the day to discourage sleeping. These rooms had their regulars, some making proper use of the periodicals, some unemployed who came to look at the jobs vacant columns of newspapers, some tramps who only came on wet or cold days, spending the warm weather in public parks.

Uniformed attendants mostly looked after the newspaper rooms but the reference librarian was responsible for ordering, receiving and checking the papers and magazines and might occasionally be called to reinforce the attendant's authority in a crisis. This would usually be the ejection of a particularly unsavoury tramp or the delivery of a reprimand to someone who had been eating, sleeping or smoking, all forbidden by the by-laws. My first experience of censorship came when I was appointed a senior assistant in a library with a newspaper room; I found that, on the specific instructions of the libraries committee, we were required to black out the betting news in the evening newspapers. This seemed to be a somewhat puritanical measure but, on inquiring the reason, I gathered that there was no moral objection to betting news but a practical one. The attendant attempting to put the evening papers on their slopes used to get mobbed by punters eager to count their gains and losses. It was not the attendant's complaints, by the way, that had led to the ban: it was the damage to the newspapers which sometimes were torn to pieces in the fracas. The attendant was an ex-master-at-arms in the Royal Navy and he regretted the loss of his one remaining legal opportunity of being involved in a scrap.

One disadvantage of the old institutional kind of reading room was its effect in keeping ladies from using it, unless it was unusually well supervised. This problem must have existed in the very early days of public libraries, when reading rooms were often the major provision, even more highly regarded than lending departments. The original solution was to have a separate ladies' reading room, thus further emphasising a separate kind of culture as few magazines were duplicated but were rather allocated to rooms according to the librarian's assessment of their interest to one sex or the other. In 1886 Thomas Greenwood, a pioneer of libraries, urged that the separate rooms for ladies should be abolished, and that separate tables in the main room be provided instead. He offered two reasons to justify the change and I wonder which influenced him most: the presence of ladies 'in a large room aids the general decorum and gives an appearance of cheerfulness and brightness . . .' and, moreover, the separate ladies' room often meant 'a good deal of gossip and sometimes it is from these rooms that fashion plates and sheets from the monthlies are most missed'.

LOCAL HISTORY

This small piece of history reminds me that I have deliberately excluded inquiries about local history from the examples given earlier in this chapter because, while reference departments have been acquiring periodicals from the disappearing newsroom, they have been losing their local history collections. In small libraries local history was the responsibility of the reference librarian, indeed the chief usually took a strong personal interest in this subject. With the amalgamation of local authorities into larger units, more and more libraries are setting up separate departments for local history and archives. This is a very welcome change because the need to preserve the material justifies special provision such as air-conditioned rooms with firedoors and burglar-proof windows and doors.

In this field public libraries make an important contribution to scholarship and research as the collections include original source material as well as printed works. The archivist or local history librarian naturally tries to obtain any books, reports or pamphlets which are relevant to the area covered and to these must be added maps, prints, photographs, paintings and anything else which assists in building up a picture of the locality. This means a responsibility for buying historical items which happen to come on the market and, incidentally, accepting gifts which often supplement the other holdings. It also means being alert to modern developments because new roads in rural areas or large-scale rebuilding in towns can change the face of the familiar scene in a very short time. What has been there in the past must be traced from the records and what is likely to disappear today must be photographed or captured in some other way for the historian of the future. The physical scene is not the only interest, for many people want to know how their forebears lived. Letters, contracts, bills of sale, title deeds, all contribute to attempts to understand a way of life. Today it is possible to secure a more vivid picture with the cine-camera and a more human one by tape-recording interviews with old people about their early life and experience in the locality.

More than any other kind of librarian, local history staffs take positive action to create their own records but they still keep the responsibility for preserving what exists. Documents and other materials which the originators expected to be ephemeral have been preserved for hundreds of years but constant inspection is needed if one is to spot signs of deterioration in time to remedy it. Public libraries of quite modest size have staff trained to repair and preserve their unique records, a task made much easier by modern technical developments such as air-conditioning and humidity control. Wear and tear of fragile original documents can be reduced by making microfilms or other photocopies and local history librarians acquire a deep knowledge of all these technical matters.

Acquiring and preserving material is only the first part of the job. Each item must be recorded and its contents indexed so that all the pieces of information relevant to an inquiry can be produced in a reasonable time. Classification has to be very detailed with lots of cross-references because local facts are needed in various contexts. A church, for instance, might interest one inquirer because he is studying all the churches in the area, another because it is an example of the architecture of a particular period or style, and a third because he is an historian studying the development of the street in which it stands. Indexing must be sophisticated enough to reveal all these facets and many more: the work of a named builder, the use of particular materials, especially local ones; developments due to a named landowner or architect. Local history librarians want to know not only what is on a site today but what was there before that, a problem often complicated by the separation of large sites into several small ones or vice versa. Names of houses are changed over the years and, in towns, house numbers have sometimes been altered as an area becomes fully built up, thus causing great confusion to the researcher who is less than meticulous.

Inquiries about local history can be very general, such as those about the development of railways in an area or about the break up of a great estate. Often a request is very specific, usually restricted to a particular site or a named person. Business executives often show great interest in the earlier history of the ground on which their offices stand and they sometimes want early prints to reproduce in a staff magazine. Special occasions such as centenaries also turn people's minds back to what things looked like in the past and church magazines, local newspapers and brochures of all kinds will be found to have an acknowledgement of help from a local history librarian. Individuals are also interested in the sites of their homes or in their ancestry. British librarians receive a steady stream of correspondence from Americans trying to piece together their family history or to establish the truth of a legend that an ancestor lived in a particular place or left it at a stated time. Inquiries of this kind are not difficult but they can be very time consuming if the information given to start with is indefinite. For instance, if one is asked a question which involves checking the parish register for a specified date to find out who was baptised, married or buried on that day there is no problem but inquirers rarely have the exact date. They are much more likely to ask when such and such a person died and can offer only approximate dates between which the event happened. If he was important enough, the local newspaper may have carried an announcement, otherwise a prolonged search of the registers may be the only way of tracing the facts.

Librarians have to use all kinds of material to answer inquiries about buildings. The date when a particular road or area was developed can be fixed approximately by the first time it appears on a map. If there are fifty years between the dates of the maps of the area the range has to be narrowed by other means, perhaps by inspecting paintings or prints which appeared between the dates. For more recent houses, the rate books record when rates were first paid and give the names of the owners or occupiers. The rate books, however, often cover a limited period in each volume and the contents are arranged by streets and houses, so that an inquiry which asks who lived at a particular address is easy to answer but one asking when a named person lived in a given house, street or area may mean days of work.

Few public librarians escape the fascination of local history. Most of us have taken part in the kind of detective work it involves and enjoy working with the members of local history and amenity societies. Usually they are prepared to undertake a lot of work themselves but they are always appreciative of any advice and guidance given by librarians. In my experience local historians are amongst the most pleasant clients librarians have, and this applies to those who may make quite casual inquiries and have no pretensions to be historians. The most satisfied inquirer I can remember was a rector who was very proud of his church's history. It had been much restored but still retained some parts of the original Norman structure; moreover, the parish could trace an unbroken line of rectors back for nearly nine hundred years. The rector had become involved in an argument with the incumbent of another parish who, whilst admitting that his own church was later than the Norman period, believed it replaced an even earlier one, thus giving his parish the seniority. I am not sure whether our rector was seeking the truth in a scholarly way or whether he merely wanted ammunition for his argument but he was finally contented when it was found that Domesday Book recorded of his parish: 'There hath always been a church at this place.'

CHAPTER FOUR

Behind the Scenes

At the end of World War II there were about 500 independent library systems in England and Wales. Some of them were in great cities with well-established libraries and some were controlled by county councils but the majority were the libraries of boroughs and urban districts with more limited responsibilities. Today the whole pattern has been changed. In 1965 Greater London government was reorganised into a smaller number of large boroughs and, in April 1974, sweeping changes were made in the rest of the country. As a result of all the redrawing of boundaries there are now fewer than 120 separate library systems, the average population served is about half a million and even the smallest authorities serve around 200,000.

Life in the public departments has not changed very much. There are more specialists to give support to the librarians serving the public and the book service has improved because more requests can be met from the resources of a large system. Nevertheless, the same borrowers are using the same branch library without caring very much that it is now a branch of Y public libraries instead of X. The same kind of questions are still being asked in reference departments, the same children listen spellbound during story hours. Local studies are becoming more specialised because the areas covered are much larger so that local history, like local government, has a new meaning and is now concerned with more than an immediate, familiar neighbourhood. There are some signs that music and gramophone record libraries are also being made grander, some of them blossoming into audio-visual departments, but these changes are very gradual.

The real revolution has taken place behind the scenes. A few years ago it was possible for one librarian to catalogue all the titles added to the stock of a small library and he might still have time to do occasional relief duty in the reference library as well. Now we have grand titles such as 'bibliographical services officer' to describe a librarian controlling fifteen, twenty, or even more staff engaged in acquiring and processing books for all the libraries in a large system. One group, headed by a stock editor, deals with ordering new titles, replacements and special requests; others classify and catalogue all the acquisitions, whilst a third section traces requests and organises inter-library loans. Many hundreds of volumes are handled every day in these departments and the librarian in charge needs to be a first-class organiser to prevent bottlenecks. The flow of books despatched to the various departments and branches must keep pace with the relentless arrival of yet more parcels.

Only the main organisation is really different. An individual cataloguer still has the same code of practice to apply to the complexities of English and foreign names. Books still have misleading titles to trap the unwary classifier. Meticulous accuracy and consistency are still expected from all the staff in the department. There are, however, more jobs for clerical workers because more titles are ordered in quantity and the cataloguer's skill is needed only for the first copy. The rest of the ten, twenty or even hundred copies can be recorded against the same master catalogue entry. The effect of this kind of change should be to achieve an overall saving which an administrator would call an economy of scale. Further possibilities for specialising within the department are beginning to be explored but the very large authorities outside London are so new that I would hesitate to say that their present ways of working are going to continue.

ORGANISATION

Most libraries now have a group of departmental heads ranking with the head of bibliographical services. These include librarians responsible for one section in the system, such as the reference libraries, the adult lending libraries, or children's work. The systems covering large geographical areas have also split their administration into divisions and smaller sections, each controlling a group of libraries. These changes are having a marked effect on the promotion prospects of librarians; comparatively few will now reach the dizzy height of becoming chief librarian of a system but many lesser peaks have been created just below the mountain tops. This brings some advantages because the librarian who has always specialised in reference work or in children's libraries can remain in that chosen field and still command a salary and a responsibility comparable with that of the former chief librarian of a small- or even medium-sized library.

The chiefs of the larger systems are becoming more and more like administrators and less and less like librarians. Sophisticated systems of management are being adopted by the new authorities but many of them are not sure where libraries fit in. Some have treated them as part of education and their chief librarians report to the director of education who is one of the main management team of the authority. Others have appointed directors of leisure whose responsibilities include libraries and, as libraries are the largest commitment, a librarian has been given the director's post in many cases. I was tempted to say 'a former librarian' has been given the post because those who accept such jobs are no longer responsible for the day-to-day running of a library. The luckiest ones are those who have been made directors but have retained libraries as their main duty, becoming directors of libraries and arts.

Whatever his title may be, the librarian of today cannot exercise the close personal control of every detail of his system as chief librarians did in the past. He is in danger of becoming a remote figure to the majority of the staff and he relies on his heads of services and his branch librarians to project his views to their colleagues. Presumably, the difficulties involved in inspiring a large and scattered staff are much the same in libraries, schools and in private industry. Every manager or director has to develop relationships with subordinates so that the vital decisions come to him and the routine ones are taken by people in whom he has confidence and who understand his general policy. In the public services, the standard problems of management are interwoven with the need to be constantly aware of the reactions of the general public. There are areas of special sensitivity in any community and the chief officers of the local authority must be aware of them and avoid allowing subordinates to take decisions which have to be overruled later.

Besides dealings with his own staff, the librarian has many concerns which involve other departments of his council. Any legal matters affecting libraries are referred to the legal section of the town clerk's department, which is also concerned with the drafting of rules, regulations and by-laws. The treasurer and his staff are responsible for most of the book-keeping and arrange payments of accounts certified in the libraries department. Providing a new branch library will involve discussions with the planning officer regarding suitable sites, co-operation from the town clerk's staff in acquiring the site eventually allocated, financing arrangements by the treasurer and, finally, detailed work on designs drawn up by the borough architect. It would be unrealistic to expect every local authority to appoint men from such a variety of professions and find they made a united and co-operative team. Inevitably, some chief officers are less competent than others, some are friendly and some unsociable, some are too involved in detail and some are jealous about their own precise position in the hierarchy.

Fortunately there are few occasions when departments are in any way competing with each other. There is no kudos for anyone in producing a branch library which is less than a credit to the town and every incentive exists for them to work together to gain a good result. Most chief officers I have worked with have been genuinely concerned about the efficiency of their departments and have had a strong social conscience about their duty to the community. Senior officers often meet at civic functions and on other social occasions and they are frequently on terms of personal friendship.

In the new authorities it seems likely that public libraries will be much more a part of local government within a framework of management systems, project co-ordination, programme planning and all the other sophistications of modern administration. I am not quite sure that I like all the changes but, like many of my colleagues, I go along with them (sometimes with tongue in cheek) to obtain an adequate share of local resources for the library service. In the early days of libraries they were rather more detached from the main stream of town-hall planning but much less money was available. Before 1919 there was a statutory limitation on the amount that could be spent on public libraries and, in order to avoid any inadvertent subsidising of library activities, the accounts were kept separately from the other departments. Library staff, like teachers, did not think of themselves as local government officers.

It was not unknown for the chief librarian to be provided with a flat over the library so that the service was virtually under his supervision both by day and night. People worked much longer hours in those days but the pace was slower and the resident librarian probably regarded himself as 'on call' rather than available in his office for much of the working day. One librarian who had enjoyed a resident post later secured a more highly paid job which did not include a flat and he found it a great hardship to go without the hot midday meal his wife used to provide. He solved the problem by showing great concern for the welfare of his staff. He repeatedly pointed out to the libraries committee that the gas ring in the staff room was quite inadequate for their needs and a proper gas cooker ought to be provided. Eventually he succeeded in installing this amenity and, thereafter, the first question asked of any applicant for a junior appointment was: 'Have you any experience of cooking?' (He proved to be a shrewd buyer of cookers because this item was still in working order when it was regretfully disposed of 40 years later because of extensive building operations to modernise the library.)

THE BUDGET

The restrictions on library expenditure led to a kind of uniformity because everyone spent the full amount allowed. Even after 1919 it took a little time for development plans to mature and, five years later, the majority of library authorities were spending a shilling (5p) per head of population per annum. Gradually, however, the councils which had always wanted to do more began to improve their services whilst others left things as they were. The most noticeable feature of the interwar years was the extraordinary variety of standards which developed, from the grossly inadequate, through the mediocre to the excellent. Surveys made during and soon after World War II showed the most advanced spending three and a half times as much as the laggards.

New legislation in 1964 gave the government powers to enforce minimum standards and librarians hoped for a gradual levelling up. Perhaps the most backward have improved their libraries but the gaps have continued to grow. In 1971–2 one council was spending 60p per head although the average for England and Wales was £1·25. In London the average figure was £2·12 per head and the highest expenditure was over £5. The sad thing is that the lowest spenders are often making their savings on book expenditure because many overheads such as building costs and staff salaries are less easy to cut. The average proportion of expenditure going on books is low enough: in 1971–2 it was approximately 25 per cent, nearly £15 million out of a total for England and Wales of £60 million.

In spite of the anomalies the average standards did rise gradually after the Act of 1919. Public libraries had to be accepted on the same basis as the other departments of local government and even the lowest budgets, if not exactly generous, at least became more realistic. Most libraries were small enough for the chief librarian to maintain a close personal control. He appointed most of the staff himself, he had a detailed knowledge of the condition of the library buildings in his care and he was closely informed on all aspects of finance. He almost certainly took the final decisions on book selection and on allocations of books to branches and departments.

Such branches were small and they were few in number until demand increased enormously after World War II. In the 1930s, most municipal chief librarians were concerned with one main library. Usually this was built in the Carnegie era and conformed to a recognisable pattern. The popular newsroom and lending library were on the ground floor and the reference department shared the upper level with the chief's office, staff workrooms and a rest-room. For some reason these buildings (many are still in use) had quite magnificent staircases which provided wall space for local prints, the borough coat-of-arms and other items of interest. The reference library was often under-used but the nearness of the offices must have been a trial to successive reference librarians, unduly overlooked by the chief librarian on his comings and goings. Southend central library went one better (or worse) than this; a small window was set in the wall outside the chief's office giving a view of the lending library counter. A visitor being shown round with me said it reminded her of childhood fears of God looking down on her every action.

George Roebuck, chief librarian of Walthamstow in the 1930s, once regretted taking so much interest in his reference library. As he paused at the entrance an enormous Irish navvy came up and put a massive arm across his shoulders:

> It was like being restrained by a bear. He asked if I was anything to do with this 'ere place. After careful reflection, I diffidently admitted that I was. In a stage whisper he said he wanted some books on 'contraption'.

It was Roebuck who once told the Essex Guild of Librarians of the great ambitions he had when he was appointed to his job. He was sure he would persuade the committee to spend twice as much on books. He was determined that, before long, his staff would enjoy the best working hours and conditions in the country. And, he added, 'everyone would say that's because Roebuck got the job'. He then mentioned all the constraints that, in practice, limit one's ambitions and implied that the individual's influence was small. In this I think he was wrong.

APPOINTMENTS AND PROMOTION

Local authorities take immense trouble over appointing chief officers. Usually the officers appointed are in their forties and have little incentive to move again until they retire twenty years or so later. It is therefore quite an event for a council to have the opportunity to make such appointments. Procedures are decided by the authority concerned but the final decision is always taken by the full council, either by approving a recommendation of an appointments committee or by interviewing several candidates chosen by the committee from a preliminary selection of ten or twelve. Appearing before the full council, if it maintains all the traditions, is quite a memorable experience. The mayor and aldermen wear their scarlet robes, the town clerk his wig and gown and the mace-bearer his best uniform and most solemn demeanour. To avoid causing any delay in the council's proceedings, the candidates are invited to attend at the town hall long before their item on the agenda is likely to be reached and they wait in an anteroom. Usually they all know each other because librarianship is a relatively small profession and candidates of the same age group have probably met from time to time when applying for more lowly jobs on their way to the top. In any case they will have met at the preliminary contest.

The first interview was the real test of their experience and professional competence and they have already answered the searching questions about their views on book expenditure, staffing standards and book-issue methods. The council is choosing a personality from two or three people who have already been thoroughly checked for their suitability, even including a medical examination. A common procedure is for each candidate to be invited to address the council for a specified period and then to answer questions. When each has had his turn and returned to the waiting room the mayor takes a vote or, sometimes, a series of votes. A clear majority is required for the appointment and if there are three or more candidates this may not be achieved at the first count, so the name with the lowest number of votes is deleted and a fresh vote taken on the remainder. The various votes are not recorded in the council minutes. The procedure is for the mayor, having announced the winner, to take a further vote on a formal motion that the named person be appointed and this is carried unanimously.

Eventually one successful and two disappointed librarians will leave the town hall, probably making for the nearest bar where the victor will console the vanquished. Already he will be thinking about looking for a house in the locality, wondering what difficult decisions have been deferred for his attention and contemplating his first meetings as a chief librarian with his staff and, later, with the libraries committee. The masculine pronoun is appropriate because a high proportion of the chief officer posts go to men, the preponderance of women recruits to librarianship being more than balanced by their earlier loss to the profession at marriage or motherhood. Women who return to work later are handicapped by the gap in their experience but, for those who stay on, the chances of promotion do not seem to be very different for men or women. Personal freedom to move to new localities in order to get promotion is important since the public librarian who hopes to become a chief officer needs to be a deputy within fifteen years or so after qualifying. This allows a few years' experience at that stage before applications are made for the top jobs, which become less and less likely of attainment after the age of forty-five.

I doubt if many newly qualified librarians have any positive ambition about being promoted. They often want to move from department to department or from library to library to gain wide experience of all aspects of their profession just for their own satisfaction. In time something happens to arouse interest in the possibilities of promotion; the event may be simply a domestic change which makes them want or need a higher salary but, more often, it is the occurrence of a vacancy on the next higher scale. A post at this level is normally filled by inviting applications from the existing staff in the basic grade.

In the enlarged libraries of today, with their widely scattered staffs, it may be difficult for anyone outside the central administration to have a good idea of the likely applicants for promotion. This is a pity because staffroom gossip has been greatly enriched in the past by attempts to assess the chances of the possible moves. A disadvantage of the very senior posts (deputy or chief librarian) is the tradition which excludes one from taking coffee or tea breaks in the staffroom. When I became a deputy it was gently pointed out that in future, tea would be brought to me at my desk because, said the chief, free speech might be inhibited by my presence in the staffroom. What most of the junior staff probably envy as a privilege of office is, for most, a penalty.

Because of this exclusion, the chief librarian who interviews the candidates and makes the appointment is often the last person to identify the winner. Whatever the result, the conversations have made many of the assistants interested in the idea of promotion; some wait for the next vacancy in their own library but others begin to scan the professional press and literary periodicals for announcements of posts for librarians. Fairly rapid advancement is possible up to the level of branch librarian. There is an assistant branch librarian for every two or three posts in the basic grade so this first step takes a few years. There is a branch librarian for each assistant branch librarian, of course, so the next move is on a one for one basis but it may take a few more years because above this level the pyramid of the organisation narrows sharply. The same is true for reference librarians and children's librarians because the supervisory posts covering the whole system are the ultimate move for many of their occupants. Fortunately not every librarian wants to rise to this level because he is then beginning to do more administration and rather less librarianship. Administration does not, however, really become a large factor, certainly not a predominant one, until one becomes a chief assistant or deputy chief librarian.

Continuing in the basic practice which was the original attraction to the profession or aiming at promotion to a post involving so much management is a difficult choice. Teachers must face a similar problem in their careers when they realise how rarely they will be in the classroom if they become headteachers. In the case of librarianship the most difficult move is the one to a post as deputy chief librarian, especially if the appointment is achieved in open competition at a strange library. Internal promotion is a little easier, as the personalities and general conditions are known; it is essential that a deputy gets on well with his chief and he can be confident of this if they are already acquainted. Other members of the staff may suffer some unhappiness if they are serving a chief whom they dislike or disagree with but at least they do not have to see him every day, most of their contacts being with the rest of the staff or with the library users. The deputy is much more closely involved in his chief's approach to policy and, if their outlooks are out of harmony, the situation is unpleasant. Fortunately, at this level, promotion is again on a 'one for one' basis and the chances of a further move for the deputy are reasonably good.

THE LIBRARIAN AND HIS COMMITTEE

The chief's work of administration is of a rather different kind from the routine day-to-day running of the system which falls to the deputy and principal assistant. He is much more involved with councillors and with committee work and he is likely to have many more contacts outside the library but connected with its work. The libraries committee is appointed by the local authority from amongst its members or it may be a sub-committee of an education committee or one dealing with leisure activities. In most cases the libraries committee has most of the powers and duties of the main authority delegated to it. It meets at regular intervals (monthly, bi-monthly or even quarterly) to decide matters of policy, approve estimates of expenditure and to consider reports put before it by the chief librarian and other officers of the council.

In theory, the committee's task is to lay down policy and the librarian's duty is to act as executive officer carrying out the policy and dealing with all the administration of the libraries. In practice, policy and administration are not always easy to separate, even though there are various legal enactments providing some guidance and each council also has its standing orders. The rules tend to acquire the permanence of the laws of the Medes and the Persians but the circumstances to which they have to be applied are constantly altering. In 1965 an important London borough still had a paper requirement that its chief officers, 'shall take steps to ensure that no bearing, hame or bridle reins shall be used on any horses belonging to or used directly or indirectly by their departments'.

A new chief librarian may be lucky enough to avoid any difficult decisions whilst he is settling in to his job but he soon has to attend a meeting of the committee. He is already familiar with the procedure because, during his time as a deputy, he sat next to his chief to proffer reports, sheets of statistics, copies of regulations or whatever other material was needed. However, all the reports are in the name of the chief officer and all the questions or requests for advice are addressed to him. As a deputy, he had to suffer in silence whilst the chief failed to make the best of a good case or floundered hopelessly with a simple question. Now, at last, he has the chance to demonstrate the perfect committee manner. The members will want to be tolerant during the first few meetings whilst the new man is finding his feet but the business has to be dealt with and they have a duty to question any points on which they are not satisfied. Very soon a working relationship is established.

Councillors regard themselves as watchdogs for the citizen's interests and, quite rightly, draw attention to any failures in administration which may come to their notice. Some try to go beyond this and interfere more than is wise in the organisation. On his side, the chief librarian may have strong views on aspects of policy which are properly the province of the committee. He is bound to be involved in the policy-making function because, whether proposals come from the committee, the chairman or the general public, the librarian is expected to report on the practical aspects such as costs, staffing requirements and any administration problems involved. Often, however, ideas for developing the service come from professional reading, attendance at conferences or meetings of staff and the librarian is then involved in initiating policy.

The precise 'balance of power' between an officer and his committee could be a fascinating study in psychology. The committee has most of the legal power and the librarian has the professional knowledge and experience. The useful harnessing of the two frequently depends on the skill and political experience of the committee chairman and thus the personalities involved may count for much more than the rules. Those who have not worked in the public services find it difficult to grasp the relationship between the salaried officer and the unpaid, elected representatives who serve on the council and its committees. The members represent the local community which pays for the library so there is, in a sense, an employee/employer relationship. Chief officers are, however, appointed by a separate committee or by the full council so the libraries committee is not directly involved. It neither appoints the officer nor fixes his conditions of service; moreover, the librarian may hold his office for twenty years or more whilst a councillor may serve on a specific committee for only two or three years.

Security of tenure for public officials has a long tradition in the British civil service and also in local government employment, having as its basis the need to protect officers from victimisation if a change of political control occurs at an election. This is a necessary safeguard but some observers consider that security has been carried too far and it is more difficult than it should be to remove from office those who are inefficient. The present system does, however, reduce any temptation for the officer to tell the committee what it wants to hear. He does not have to be very courageous to give honest advice, even if he expects it to be unpalatable.

The views of the librarian and the committee are not often in conflict on major matters; in my own experience they have frequently been on the same side in trying to persuade the finance committee to vote more money for books or the staff committee to agree to provide for an expanding service. Committee members naturally attach much importance to things they can see for themselves: a reference library which happens to be half empty when a member visits it for a few minutes may be regarded as an extravagance unless the librarian is convincing in reporting its heavy use at other times. Many a librarian has tried in vain to abolish a newspaper reading room in favour of an enlarged lending department serving far more people who are, however, taking their books home to read. The most frustrating aspect of committee work for the inexperienced is the way attitudes change from one meeting to the next, particularly if a persuasive member is present at one of the meetings and absent from the other.

Sometimes a policy is agreed on one occasion but the practical measures to implement it are rejected later on. For instance, the committee may express concern that so many children cease to use the library after they leave school and the librarian is instructed to find ways to attract teenagers to the libraries. He recommends extending the gramophone record collection to include jazz and other popular music but the proposal is rejected. He then suggests subscribing to periodicals which appeal to young people but is unwise enough to bring some specimen copies for the committee to see; after looking at the illustrations they coldly say no. In desperation the librarian offers to arrange coffee evenings for local youth groups so that they can be shown the library facilities which might interest them. The few committee members who supported the first two suggestions gleefully point out that the majority has just decided to do nothing for teenagers and there is no point in bringing them to the library to tell them so. By this time the chairman is becoming tired of the subject and passes on to the next item on the agenda without taking a vote.

In these rare instances of disagreement, the committee's power is decisive in the short term but, as the membership changes over the years, the librarian may be able to influence policy in a different direction later on. The librarian is also, in many instances, expressing views which are a synthesis of those of his colleagues. In the longer term a form of departmental policy is developed in large systems which has great influence. This is going to be even more important in the future as the very large organisation has a kind of momentum of its own and it is very difficult for a spot decision in a committee to have much permanent effect. The long-term planning of the service is a different matter for the committee can make real policy decisions on capital expenditure which will affect the future.

OTHER SYSTEMS OF CONTROL

The position of the chief librarian in the United States has many similarities with that of his British colleagues. He is the adviser to a lay board which, theoretically, is concerned with overall policy. Most of the finance for the library is provided by the city or other local taxation authority and most, if not all, the members of the board are appointed locally, perhaps by the mayor. The board is, however, an independent organisation and provides within the librarian's control the general administration which, in England, would be available from other local authority departments. The members of the board often remain in office for many years and this may tend to give them a stronger control of policy but, as they do not have to seek re-election, they may not always be so representative of the local population.

In other parts of the world the British system has been adapted to meet local needs. In Australia, for instance, the State governments had set up public libraries in their capitals before the Federal government was formed in 1910 and the State influence has remained to encourage development in the sparsely populated areas. One therefore finds locally controlled libraries with their own chief librarians on the British pattern but having access to a headquarters organisation and reference service governed by the State library boards. Canadian city libraries are generally invested in library boards, as in the United States, but the boards include members of the city council and are closer to the municipality giving them some of the advantages of the British system. In all the various systems one always finds a committee of some kind responsible for policy and a professional librarian advising and dealing with the daily running of the service.

PROFESSIONAL ASSOCIATIONS

A librarian's own ideas can be expressed most freely to the colleagues he meets through professional associations, regional co-operation groups, working parties and all the committees and sub-committees which seem to proliferate in a modern society. Regional associations such as the Association of London Chief Librarians and its predecessor the Association of Metropolitan Chief Librarians have greatly improved library services by voluntary agreement. In London it is possible to obtain a membership card at a local library which will be accepted anywhere in the Greater London area, an arrangement made by the chief librarians and recommended to their committees. The London librarians also maintain a stock specialisation scheme whereby each accepts responsibility for buying at least one copy of every British book in a specified subject area so that complete coverage is provided by the combined effort. The scheme has always been supplemented by a parallel system for fiction and it has recently been extended to include sound recordings.

The national associations have regular conferences which provide opportunities for the exchange of views and they also include a number of social gatherings, when the conversation invariably turns to the subject of books and libraries. The printed Conference Proceedings, together with the monthly *Library Association Record*, provide a conspectus of librarians' views covering nearly a hundred years.

Some surprisingly vigorous arguments have been conducted and a number of men are still recalled because of their association with particular policies. Alfred Cotgreave (1849–1911) is remembered as the inventor of a new type of 'indicator' for closed-access libraries but he was a bitter campaigner against open access, which did away with indicators altogether. It was perhaps unfortunate that Cotgreave found himself librarian of West Ham in the late 1890s because open access began a few miles away at Clerkenwell in 1894 under the energetic J. Duff Brown. Brown had many other interests, for he also produced a complete subject classification incorporating some very original ideas and was responsible for the basic *Manual of Library Economy* (1903) which has survived through successive revisions until the present day.

Some controversies continue through the years. Questions of staff training and the syllabus for examinations are always good for an argument but this, of course, is not confined to chief librarians for the Association of Assistant Librarians has much to say on these subjects, as indeed it has on many others. The recreational use of libraries is a recurring topic; should 'light' fiction be stocked at all at the public expense? Censorship is considered from time to time, although few are likely to find their views changed after the discussion. Because there are so many different types of library it is not surprising that the organisation of the profession is constantly in question and not infrequently being readjusted.

Although librarians try to be impartial in book selection and in the application of techniques such as classification, they often hold strong views about their work. Rightly or wrongly, branch librarians express something of their personalities in the way they run their branches and chiefs do the same for whole systems. Some have a particular interest in providing services to the sick or the handicapped, others will want to develop work with children and yet others will inaugurate collections of sound recordings, pictures and other non-book materials. Even where decisions have to be taken by a committee, the report must be written by the librarian and, in spite of all attempts to be neutral and to state the facts impartially, the predilections of the writer usually have their influence. Committees like to have a positive recommendation which helps to focus discussion but management experts might deprecate this personal influence and claim that professional enthusiasm should not be allowed to interfere with objectivity in reports. They may be right but, as one of the professionals, I cannot believe that libraries can be lively and interesting places unless they are run by lively and interesting people who find it hard to suppress their views. Without a positive attitude at the top, libraries will become dull institutional book stores.

CHAPTER FIVE

Ideals and Realities

Young librarians complain that far too much library literature deals with controversies about processes and techniques and very little is said on ideals, purposes and philosophy. I suspect this point of view is a reaction by people who have a long period of education and academic training and then find themselves in a working situation which does not, at first, provide the right kind of challenge. Many older librarians were trained, as apprentices are, working in libraries and either doing their theoretical study on a part-time basis or eventually being granted leave of absence to complete their examinations. They took the essential routine work in their stride, were very practical in their outlook and assumed that the end result (more books lent, more inquiries answered) was self-evidently a good thing.

I remember, in my first job at a branch library, the interest we all took in the daily record of books issued and the sense of achievement when the figure first exceeded 1,000 items on a busy Saturday. As we were not paid by results I suppose we could have regretted the increase, which gave us nothing but a harder day's work; instead, we were very pleased. We could, I suppose, have wondered whether all the books taken out would actually be read from cover to cover. We could have wondered whether the people concerned really ought to spend their time reading or whether it would be better for them to do something else.

Untroubled by such misgivings, most librarians have concentrated on making libraries available to everyone, siting them in the best places, opening them at times when readers could use them and setting very wide limits to the range of material stocked. The objectors could claim that it is impossible to give a good service if one tries to be all things to all men with only limited resources. However, a number of statements from respected sources gives guidance on principles, even for the very wide purposes of the public library. For many senior librarians there is more need to live up to the ideals already formulated than to discuss new ones.

Ideals and philosophies are relevant if resources are more than usually restricted and the librarian has to choose between meeting all the educational demands by severely limiting recreational material or trying to keep some sort of balance between all the possible uses. Lionel McColvin, formerly city librarian of Westminster, once discussed the possibility of a points system in selection. A very light novel might have one point for literary merit and ten for popular demand, whereas a learned work might reverse these scores and still achieve the same total mark in the assessment. Unfortunately, the merit mark involves a value judgement which would not secure universal agreement and the librarian is back where he started.

The Public Libraries and Museums Act of 1964 defines the duty of a library authority as the provision of a 'comprehensive and efficient library service for all persons desiring to make use thereof'. Section 7(2) of the Act expands the definition by referring to adequate stocks and mentions books and other materials 'sufficient in number, range and quality to meet the general requirements and any special requirements'. This is ample authority for librarians who insist that their duty involves all types of demand and educational needs should not be given priority. Indeed, the first Public Libraries Act for England and Wales (1850) specifically refers to 'recreation' in its preamble. The sponsors are widely believed to have cherished the hope that drunkenness would be reduced because the working man would have less time for drinking if he spent some part of his leisure in recreational reading. Progress has been made since then: in a recent debate on censorship a member of parliament expressed the view that young people would be doing less harm if they stayed at home and read a little light pornography on public holidays instead of invading seaside places where they obstructed the police and annoyed the local residents.

CENSORSHIP

Should public libraries provide pornography? Whenever a librarian is asked about his book selection policy the question of censorship is bound to arise. Not all librarians regard this as the most important problem in the choices they have to make but it is an emotive one which cannot be ignored. Many of us meet colleagues from other countries and are aware that censorship is applied very differently in different places. Some communities deal harshly with librarians who provide a balanced stock showing all points of view on social and political questions. In one country they must exclude anything which glorifies communism whilst in another they must exclude anything which opposes it. Support for racial segregation is illegal in one place and support for integration is a crime in another. Religion obviously has its dangers as a subject for writers but the sensitivity of governments varies from place to place and also from century to century. Sexual matters have had the longest run of all the possible subjects for censorship but, again, the intensity of the objections has been noticeably varied in different countries. Sex is only now in some danger of being displaced by a more vocal disapproval of violence in literature.

What is the librarian's duty in the matter of censorship? As ordinary citizens many of us may have strong views on the subjects which have been mentioned above and, like our neighbours, we may approve or disapprove of some form of censorship. Long experience in dealing with books and people possibly gives librarians a clearer insight into the real issues than is commonly available and they might be regarded as expert witnesses on the subject. However, when matters of religion or morals are under discussion few people in a democratic society really want to listen to balanced views from experts. In his day-to-day duty the librarian is not concerned about what the law of his country ought to be; even if, in his private capacity, he campaigns to change the law he must still uphold it in his work. The problem for the public librarian is almost invariably how to prevent a local community from imposing a book selection policy which is more restrictive than that required by the law of the land.

The professional ideal for British librarians has been clearly stated by the Library Association which holds that it is the function of a library service to provide, so far as resources allow, all books, periodicals, etc, other than the trivial, in which readers claim legitimate interest. In deciding what is a legitimate interest the librarian should be guided solely by the law of the land:

> If the publication of such matter has not incurred penalties under the law, it should not be excluded from libraries on any moral, political, religious or racial ground alone, to satisfy any sectional interest. The public are entitled to rely upon libraries for access to information and enlightenment upon every field of human experience and activity. Those who provide library services should not restrict this access except by standards which are endorsed by law.

American librarians have been equally forthright in expressing their duties. In 1939 the American Library Association adopted a 'Library Bill of Rights' which has since had some minor revisions but, in relation to book selection, is substantially in line with the British view:

> In no case should library materials be excluded because of the race or nationality or the social, political, or religious views of the author . . . no library materials should be proscribed or removed from libraries because of partisan or doctrinaire disapproval.
>
> Censorship should be challenged by libraries in the maintenance of their responsibility to provide public information and enlightenment.

Librarians in all parts of the world have had many censorship 'incidents' to cope with and some have shown great courage in defending their principles. Book burning is by no means out of date and enlightenment has not yet reached the level where the vast majority of people will allow all points of view to be expressed so that, 'haply, the truth may prevail'. In America the McCarthy 'witch hunt' against communism caused many embarrassments to librarians but other forms of restriction are not unknown. As recently as 1968 the librarian of Richmond, near San Francisco, resigned because of controversy about two newspapers and a magazine which he had chosen for display in the library. The Library Board supported him but a public meeting was hostile to any manifestation of the 'underground press'.

I cannot imagine a public meeting on such a subject in Britain, partly because the people are more tolerant (or apathetic?) but more because the conflicts are less open and the librarian battles in private with the chairman of the committee or the leader of the majority political party. The objections are mostly against books which include too explicit descriptions of sexual matters but the unpublicised battles often relate to attempts by committee members to overstress political newspapers and magazines favouring their own views. The small, remote communities suffer most from these troubles but I know of cases even in central London where the choice of exhibitions permitted in a public library has been influenced by party political considerations. Fortunately, political or religious censorship of book selection is, in England and Wales, almost unknown.

However, Roman Catholics are forbidden by their church to read or keep without permission any books on a list issued by the Vatican under the formidable title 'Index Librorum Prohibitorum', generally known as the Index or Index Vaticanus. Fortunately, even this is not usually a worry for the individual librarian because, in predominantly Catholic countries such as Eire, these titles may not be printed or imported. As the works are unobtainable neither the committee nor the librarian has to make any decisions about buying them. Once or twice Irish librarians have applied in all innocence for 'listed' books through the inter-library lending system and copies sent by English libraries have been impounded by the Irish customs. Usually, after a certain amount of fuss falling somewhat short of an international incident, the books have been returned to the senders.

The librarian has to cope with constant pressure from committed groups who want their views well represented and all opposition excluded. He also has to concern himself with books which are freely available, carry no legal penalties but would offend a minority group of readers. A few librarians evade the issue by 'not selecting' controversial items. As I have said, unless funds could be unlimited there has to be selection and it is therefore possible to say that a particular book is not banned or excluded but just happened to be one that was not chosen for stock. If the book has been widely reviewed and is being asked for by readers there is no good excuse for not buying it. An admission that fear of complaints has led to the exclusion of a book is at least honest, if not very brave, but the pretence of non-selection is both cowardly and dishonest. Many librarians are tempted by another form of evasion of the ideal by keeping controversial books off the open shelves. This at least ensures that they are available for anyone who specifically demands them and avoids offence to those who might take a book casually and only later find that it is franker than they like. The problem is to ensure that genuine availability is preserved for those who want the segregated items.

There are many people who feel shy about asking for books on contraception or on sex instruction but want to read them and, if works are in the library, they are entitled to have them. The only sure way of making books available is to put them on the library shelves so that all who have the right to borrow them may see them and choose them if they wish. An apocryphal story is told of a librarian who insisted there was no censorship in his library. 'Is *Lady Chatterley's Lover* in stock?' 'Certainly it is.' 'Is it available for anyone who wants to read it?' 'Certainly it is.' Then, after a pause, 'It is locked up in my desk and freely available to anyone who has the damned effrontery to come and ask me for it.'

Books which are not likely to involve censorship problems can still involve moral dilemmas. How far should a librarian prefer quality of book use to quantity? There was a time when it was hoped that the less-educated public could be attracted to the library by the provision of western stories, detective novels and light romances and then led on to better things. Victorian confidence in a perpetual advance towards the light led to a belief that readers would eventually choose the highest when they saw it. Once they had taken the bait of light fiction, they would be influenced by the predominance of the classics and graduate to the best that was available. It would be wrong to state categorically that this never happens but few librarians today seriously hope to attract adults with trivia and expect them to be demanding Tolstoy within a few years.

Most of us are resigned to the fact that reading tastes are largely fixed in childhood and only in rare cases is there a great leap forward afterwards, although increasing discrimination within a particular area is possible. We have learnt to accept that escapist literature is wanted for its own sake and not as a stepping-stone to something else. For some reason, most public librarians accept detective stories, even of very poor quality, but are much more cautious about light romances and 'westerns'. Equally unexplained is the acceptance of light literature coupled with a rigid insistence on very high standards in the choice of sound recordings, which are often limited to works which have some claim to be classics. There are still many British libraries which refuse to stock jazz records or tapes.

The addition of 'pop' records to a London library led to a prolonged correspondence in the *Library Association Record*. 'More money than sense', 'Beatles before Beethoven', were the rallying cries of an incensed opposition from librarians who cheerfully stocked the lightest of light fiction. Strangely enough, there is some evidence that the Victorian hope of improving taste is more likely to be achieved in music than in reading, at least amongst younger adults. Perhaps 'improving' taste implies an unjustified value judgement and I should have said a widening taste, for the youngster who finds nothing he wants in the 'pop' section sometimes takes Beethoven on that occasion and later uses all sections of the stock to some extent.

I am sure we should avoid blanket disapproval of any form of literature or creative art. It is much more difficult, but nevertheless necessary, to try to exercise a reasonable discrimination within each field. Some publishers produce love stories which are at least grammatical and show a variety of settings, while others produce the same plot with new characters in the same wrongly punctuated, badly constructed text. Science fiction varies from novels with a real claim to be part of a vigorous development in English fiction to stories which are lurid rubbish. No two people will agree about all the borderline cases but a general policy of trying to stock the best in every field does have an effect on the general pattern of a library service.

CENSORSHIP AND CHILDREN

Children's librarians who accept the validity of the case for a wide provision for adults often insist that children are still malleable and must be offered only books of the highest quality. If they constantly come in contact with the best children's books they will, later in life, instinctively spurn inferior products. There is enough truth in this view to make it difficult to oppose and, as very good children's and teenagers' novels have been published in recent years, there are no practical difficulties in the way of applying the policy. Perhaps it could be hinted that one can be just a little too solemn and protective in choosing books for children. Some of them go through a period in which they are voracious readers but quite undiscriminating, turning from a comic strip to Dickens with equal enthusiasm. Usually it is the comics which are dropped eventually.

Choosing books for children occasionally has its excitements. A few librarians have made headlines in the press by refusing to stock books by Enid Blyton because some children become 'one author' readers and will take nothing except another Enid Blyton. The problem is real enough and attempts to persuade or encourage a child to try other authors are justified but a flat refusal to supply the requested book makes the whole business too important and possibly drives the child away from the library for years. Sensible comment is as unwelcome to the over-dedicated children's librarian as the doctor's advice to the young mother whose first baby was a month or two behind the average in toilet training: 'They nearly always grow out of it before the age of twenty.'

Children's librarians are nevertheless right to emphasise quality rather than quantity in library use. Because quality is difficult to measure there has always been pressure on librarians to issue the maximum number of books to the widest possible readership because these are things which can be counted and compared. Maximum use is not necessarily the best test of a library's effectiveness or even of its impact on a community. There will always be people who give other activities a higher rating than reading but still make some use of libraries and give them their support. A common-sense policy is not to attempt to recruit the entire population but rather to ensure that the service is fully available to all who want it and is known to everyone. Any who fail to use it then do so deliberately.

The pioneers of public library legislation sought to meet or anticipate the need for books which followed the spread of literacy and wider opportunities for education. A few locally supported libraries existed both in Britain and in the United States before the general movement developed in the 1840s and culminated in enabling acts about 1850. In America, the motivation was partly based on the possibilities of self-improvement; if students educated themselves with the aid of a library, rugged individualism could be applied to the choice of subjects, the amount of time spent on them and so on. In England, the campaign was part of the demand for a more formal national system of education which achieved its first successes in the founding of the Mechanics' Institutes in industrial towns. Popular education for artisans and labourers was the objective and libraries were meant to provide for self-development in an atmosphere of freedom.

Free service was at one time unacceptable to some people and the free libraries had a social stigma. They were therefore used mainly by those for whom they were originally intended, although artisans and clerks greatly outnumbered labourers. County libraries probably helped to change the status of the public library because, in small towns and villages, it was much more convenient for all classes to use the local branch rather than a subscription library some distance away. A few years after World War II, Cadness Page, the head of Harrod's book department and library, told the Society of Bookmen that he was quite shocked to see 'a nice type of person' frequenting the public library in one of the more affluent parts of Surrey. This sounds somewhat naïve but he knew his job and his observation was sound enough, for the subscription and commercial lending libraries have now almost ceased to exist. Book borrowing for all sections of the community now means borrowing from the public library, except for the use of professional association libraries and educational institutions for specific purposes. In England and Wales alone, over 600 million books are lent by public libraries every year; on a single Saturday during the winter months over 5 million books are taken home.

Many of the things which have helped in this success story have been mentioned in earlier chapters. A more progressive attitude towards work with children is one of the most important developments. Good siting of libraries, which I have also mentioned, has always been of concern to librarians but the town council has sometimes had a wrong assessment of the need. Councillors with great enthusiasm for civic affairs find a coherence in them which is not apparent to the general public. Apart from using the same source of finance there is no logical link between city halls, public baths, clinics and libraries and yet councils love to put them together as monuments to civic achievement.

The controlling authority must make it clear that the council provides the service because any aggrieved citizen must know where, in the last resort, he can make complaints. The danger in over-emphasising the municipality is that there are difficult areas in some towns where potential users are deterred by the idea of a government or local government institution. There are those who dislike, or even fear, any association with authority and worry about signing an application form for library membership. By-laws and regulations are forbidding documents to many and even the stout hearted were once deterred by the mass of notices in public libraries: 'No Smoking', 'No Dogs Allowed', 'Silence'. A few enlightened councils have been glad to be more discreet with these prohibitions but very often their librarians have had to persuade them.

THE UNDER-PRIVILEGED

The problem areas are often those of inner cities and I find hope in what has been done in America. There the problems are much greater than in Britain because the under-privileged citizens are predominantly non-whites living in areas which the Americans themselves describe as black ghettoes. If the problems are greater, so are the energies and enthusiasms being devoted to their solution. In the last year or two, any conversation I have had with visiting American librarians has included some reference to 'outreach', an expression of positive attempts to reach people instead of waiting for them to appear at the library.

Special efforts are being made to attract teenagers to libraries by offering many activities in addition to the printed word. Exhibitions, films and discussions are not unusual forms of library extension work but here they are specially related to a community need, often specifically chosen for black people. Steel-band concerts and judo classes are less likely forms of library extension but, if they bring deprived young people into a library group where they are accepted, it is difficult to criticise. Queens Borough library in New York has achieved the ultimate in informality by providing a community centre from which books are lent without any record being made. This is a worthwhile experiment to solve the problem of the social 'drop-outs' who are suspicious of requests for a name and address.

Queens Borough also has the credit for the Library-Go-Round which are brightly coloured vehicles rather like ice-cream vans with room inside for small groups who can see films, listen to records or story hours and finally take a book home. New York is not by any means the only city to have problems or to be trying to solve them; recent reports of interesting outreach projects come from Baltimore, Boston and Chicago and one could go on through the alphabet.

Concern for the under-privileged has not been limited to the home country. Young librarians occasionally volunteer to spend one or two years in a developing country before embarking on their careers at home. The organisation known as Voluntary Service Overseas arranges these appointments for British people with specific skills or qualifications. Many more librarians spend time abroad later in their careers when they have enough experience to help in the planning of nationwide systems or of large public or university libraries. Many have helped to set up schools of librarianship which, in their early stages, have to be staffed by British or American librarians. Even the stay-at-home librarians become aware of what is happening in many parts of the world because of the steady stream of librarian visitors from abroad and the frequent attachment of student librarians to their staff.

People living in countries with a long tradition of compulsory education find it difficult to enter into the lives of those who have to struggle to gain a few years' basic instruction only to find their reading ability declines later through lack of practice. Illiteracy has been widely publicised and while the efforts of international organisations to remedy it are sometimes reported, the intensity of the yearning for books which will make self-instruction possible is rarely understood. Formal schooling is now established in many areas which were completely deprived a generation ago and, in time, the length of education will be extended as it has been in more advanced countries. The libraries are the next step in development and they are essential if the previous efforts are not to be wasted.

British and American help in setting up libraries in other countries has been quietly developing for half a century. It began with services to countries which, in economic resources, were in the advanced group and has extended since the war to newly independent areas. Outside the professional journals very little has been reported about the achievements of individual librarians and of both official and voluntary organisations which have been inspired by an ideal.

Britain was in a particularly good position to help during the interwar years because her educational institutions had a long tradition of welcoming overseas students, mainly from the Commonwealth countries, and the schools of librarianship were following normal practice in accepting young people from abroad. A small but steady stream of qualified librarians returned home to practise in their own countries what they had learnt. After the war the numbers increased enormously and were supplemented by the many British librarians who worked enthusiastically to develop libraries overseas. In America, although there was no traditional traffic of dominion and colonial students, many hundreds of student librarians from other countries have been trained. Norway, in particular, established a cadre of trained personnel from American library schools. The pattern of development has been through several phases which have overlapped. Students came to Britain and America, then librarians (mainly from Britain) went abroad and, finally, library schools were set up in the developing countries. Roy Flood, of the British Council, once said that Britain's most valuable contribution was her export of librarians.

The British Council was established in 1934 and its Books Department set up libraries in many territories. Professional librarians controlled the operations and many went out from Britain to serve at the local centres. Originally the intention seemed to be no more than the provision of a chain of libraries of British books as part of the Council's general function of explaining Britain and its affairs. The success of the service led to gradual changes and the libraries became examples of a public library service which was developed in co-operation with the governments of the territories concerned. A policy decision a few years after the war shifted the emphasis from jointly controlled services to the encouragement of locally supported and controlled libraries.

Jamaica was one of the first successes of this policy and is regarded as a model. It was still a colonial territory when Hugh Paget arrived as the British Council representative. He set up a committee to look into educational needs and the report which it produced stressed the importance of a library service, fortunately coinciding with the Jamaica library survey carried out by a Canadian librarian, Nora Bateson. The first Jamaican libraries to be established following these reports came during the 1940s, when the British Council's policies generally favoured joint financing, but the shift towards independence followed quickly. A. S. A. Bryant, librarian of Nuneaton, went to Jamaica in 1948 and took charge for about five years, and both he and his successor emphasised the need to train Jamaicans. In 1955 one of them, Joyce Lawson, took over the service which was then fully operational and independent both of British finance and British manpower.

Almost any report about library development overseas makes reference to Jamaica, partly because it is a classic case of everything going according to plan but also because of the continuing friendship between Jamaican librarians and their British colleagues. Students and young librarians visit and study libraries in Britain, some of them attend conferences and usually have useful contributions to make. Already they are able to report successful extensions of their work into various cultural activities and they have begun to provide a schools' library service.

British Council librarians have repeated the story of Jamaica in a long list of countries, especially in Africa, but there are still very many places without libraries and others which cannot meet local needs and have to restrict access by charging subscriptions. Still others rely on boxes of books sent them by charities such as the Ranfurly library service. The British Council's work is mainly in the field of public libraries because the Inter University Council, which was set up to encourage the establishment of universities, included libraries in its activities. J. H. P. Pafford, who was then Goldsmiths' librarian in the University of London, was made library adviser to the council and his guidance in the selection of librarians and in the provision of advice and help 'in the field' has given excellent results.

United States aid for overseas libraries has also included direct support, starting with the American library in Paris which opened about 1920. In the 1940s the Good Neighbour policy led to library aid for many Latin American countries but long before this the Carnegie Corporation and the Rockefeller Foundation were implementing various programmes for library development in many parts of the world. In the 1950s the Ford Foundation added library support to its projects for foreign aid and, as it emphasises national and university libraries in its work, it complements the others, the Carnegie Corporation being mainly concerned with public libraries and the Rockefeller Foundation with special libraries or information centres.

The importance of all these projects to the practising librarian is the number of opportunities for travel and for taking posts overseas which they make available. All the schemes have to be implemented by librarians. Major surveys have usually been made by well-known figures in the profession who have been seconded from their normal work for a few months. Ernest Savage laid the foundations for the West Indies developments by a report prepared as far back as 1934. Lionel McColvin went to Australia for the British Council in 1946 and his successor at Westminster, K. C. Harrison, is almost a roving ambassador for British librarianship. A few reputations have been made because of work done abroad. Edward Sydney, who was librarian of a small system in East London, was known throughout the world for his services to the Unesco-Delhi Pilot Library Project, and Eve Evans, as a British Council librarian, became widely respected for her work in Ghana from 1954 onwards. This service culminated in the Ghana National Libraries Board which was set up in 1971.

Contacts today continue through the International Federation of Library Associations and through Unesco and many specialised groups. Although chief librarians are strongly represented in these groups there are many opportunities for young librarians to travel if they wish to: travelling fellowships, study tours, exchange arrangements, all add to the variety of chances. The roots of this strong international aspect of British and American librarianship lie in the early establishment of public libraries in which they were ahead of the rest of the world for perhaps a hundred years. Other countries were bound to build on this experience and, where they have caught up, they have maintained friendly contacts and, where they are still developing, they still turn to advanced systems for advice and help. There is still much to be done and the following words from the 1951 Unesco Report are as true today as when they were written: 'Over and over again children and adults in underdeveloped areas have been laboriously taught to read and write only to relapse into illiteracy through lack of library services.'

CHAPTER SIX

The Wider Public Library

From the very beginning of the public library movement there have been arguments about whether librarians should concentrate solely on books or whether they might properly arrange lectures, poetry readings and other cultural activities which seem to spring naturally from library use. Many of the statutes about libraries have included references to art galleries and museums so local authorities often group these institutions under one committee with the chief librarian in overall control of them. Most of the library staff do not need to become involved in the separate functions but the museum is bound to have a special interest for the local history librarians. Controversy has arisen mainly about 'non-book' activities based on the library itself.

Even where he is not responsible for a museum or art gallery the most book-minded librarian has usually been compelled to widen his work a little. He has rarely been able to prevent his premises being used for some community purposes, especially those which need to take place in the evenings. Libraries have always been focal points which, in towns, assume some of the functions of the village hall in rural areas. Modern legal aid, for instance, was preceded by 'the poor man's lawyer', a local solicitor who attended at the public library at regular times to give advice to those who could not afford normal professional fees. Justices of the peace operated a rota to ensure that one of them was available once or twice a week to witness documents and, again, the library was the most likely venue. It has many advantages for these ancillary uses: its location is widely known and 'the central library' is adequate as an address; it is usually sited to be accessible to most of the population of the town; above all, perhaps, it is open until eight or nine o'clock in the evening for its normal purposes. To use a church hall or school during the evening means opening it specially, arranging lighting and heating in winter and paying the caretaker at overtime rates.

Rooms provided for the non-library purposes I have mentioned are not needed all the time or even every night and they are often hired to local cultural societies for a small fee. Some librarians, quite early on, began to use them also for 'extension activities', by which they meant readings, record recitals or other small events which might encourage people to visit the library. The decision to do this seems to be very much a matter for librarians rather than committees because many of the pioneers started programmes in one place and then, on being appointed elsewhere, started all over again. One early example was the work of L. Stanley Jast, a distinguished librarian of Manchester (from 1920 to 1931) who had previously been in charge at Croydon. He made great contributions to conventional librarianship, including the introduction of the first mobile libraries, for which he used converted buses, but he was also interested in the arts. Whilst at Croydon he organised programmes of readings, lectures and concerts in the libraries and later started similar events at Manchester.

Many librarians have opposed this widening of their work. Lionel McColvin, a leader of professional thinking I mentioned in earlier chapters, held that 'the library should stick to its job'. The Library Association, possibly influenced by McColvin, gave its views in an official report in 1942: 'It is the function of the public library to provide books.' This was a fundamentalist view which held that librarians should be concerned with lectures and other adult education activities but only in so far as they could supply books or reading lists. The events themselves should be organised by someone else.

This official policy is now quite divorced from reality. It was eroded by librarians who were extremely orthodox in their views about books but wanted to encourage more people to use them. This led to lectures, which could be linked with books, and then to literary societies, poetry and drama groups and other activities specifically using the library's stocks. This all seemed very safe but, in time, the lecturers wanted to illustrate their talks with slides or filmstrips rather than books; the poetry evenings were made more attractive if the readings were interspersed with excerpts of recorded music . . . where should one stop? Eventually, if the attendances are good, the librarian is bound to change the question and ask *why* he should stop.

Despite the hesitations of many librarians and the outright opposition of some, a lot has been done in recent years. Whatever their views on widening the range of the adult library, almost all librarians have accepted the provision of films, talks and book weeks for children. It can certainly be claimed that a free film show will lure children into the library but its direct connection with the borrowing of books might be difficult to prove in many cases. The truth is that even the librarians whose heads tell them that libraries and arts are separate things for adults are not hard-hearted enough to stop their children's departments from enriching the lives of young people. Unwittingly, librarians who have accepted these things for children have ensured the future of libraries and arts together for the children are growing up to expect libraries to offer more than books. Today's children are tomorrow's adult library users and also tomorrow's councillors and committee members.

Library systems vary so much in their involvement with the arts that I cannot describe a particular programme and say it is a typical one. Many librarians have spent all their working lives in public libraries without ever being called upon to take part in extension work. Others, often from choice, have worked in libraries where every member of the staff was expected to play his part. My own experiences have been a series of contrasts, beginning with a request from the branch librarian who was my first boss to act as librarian to the weekly meetings of a branch of the Workers' Educational Association. Boxes of books were supplied partly from our own stock and partly on requisition from the central library. All I had to do was to attend the lectures and deal with the issue and return of books at the end. Subjects changed for each winter series and, whilst I was on the staff of the branch, I had one course on English literature, another on anthropology and a final one on American politics. There is no subject which is not useful knowledge for a librarian; all is grist to the mill and, after all, I was paid to attend whilst everyone else had paid to be there.

The same branch librarian helped to start a number of societies, offering a meeting place in the library and some general help with publicity, programmes and organisation, which is just the support amateur groups need. I always seemed to become involved in producing reports and programmes on a rather messy hand-operated duplicator. The smudgy results were always received with gratitude and I made some amends by being an expert with a stencil outfit used to manufacture simple posters. As a sideline to these affairs one has practice in speaking and few librarians remain inarticulate for long. There is no great strain in addressing a small group of students about returning their books on time and then it is only a short step to introduce a gramophone record recital. Within months I found myself running film shows for a vast crowd of children and soon excelled at obtaining free loans of films. Our projector was somewhat antiquated and I also had to become expert at splicing broken films almost invisibly. Members of the societies and the parents and teachers of the children soon became firm friends of the library because of these quite small extra events. Many of the staff made friends with members of societies in which they were interested but I think the most important result was the development of a strong library 'lobby' amongst influential citizens.

After a few years I moved to another library where the service was completely conventional. Although I stayed there for several years and worked both at a busy branch and at the central library I cannot recall any activity which was not directly related to the book service. Even a notice-board with details of local arts events was lacking. Perhaps I was unusual in not finding out more about libraries before applying for jobs but there were few chances of promotion in those days and one tended to apply for things within travelling distance of home. Maybe younger librarians even today apply for posts with a similar ignorance of what is in store for them but at a more senior level one learns to study annual reports and published statistics and perhaps to visit a library before applying. These precautions can be wasted if the library changes its policy.

Later on I was attracted to a library system because its conventional services were being modernised and developed very rapidly. Within a few years the main work had been reorganised but the momentum of change swept us on to start a gramophone record library and then to arrange concerts and record recitals. As the only member of staff to claim at least some experience in such matters I was soon involved, although my chief's knowledge of music was far superior to mine. On one occasion he had arranged to give a talk to the local music society on the works of Gilbert and Sullivan, with interludes of recorded music, but two days before the event an official duty of some kind intervened and, rather than cancel the talk, he prevailed on me to stand in for him. The music society usually had an attendance of about 300 members, some of them knowledgeable about most kinds of music. I had two evenings to read all I could about Gilbert and Sullivan, building on the one basic fact of knowing which was composer and which librettist because I had catalogued their works. I then gave a lecture consisting of the fewest possible words spoken by me and the longest possible excerpts from the gramophone records. The audience seemed to enjoy it.

Since those days I have worked in a library which had just abandoned its extension work as an economy measure and in another which, on paper, did nothing for the arts because there was a local arts council which received support from the borough council. In practice they leaned heavily on the library for advice, publicity and help with their box office for events. Finally, I have seen a modest scheme run by two or three librarians in their spare time grow into an impressive arts and entertainments department with a dozen experts employed full time. There really is no typical arts programme for libraries but the trend towards involvement and more professional development is unmistakable. The change in thinking, although it has been slow to develop, really began in 1948.

Before then it was sometimes necessary to stretch the meaning of the Libraries Acts to justify spending money on all the extension work and the formation of a society was one way of doing this. Although the librarian might start the society, it was an independent body, at least in theory, so that any arts activities it carried out were not officially the acts of the libraries committee or of the librarian. There could be doubt about the legal right of a local authority to show films on library premises but there was no doubt about its right to let a room to a local society for a nominal fee and the society could then show films to its members. A section of the Local Government Act of 1948 gave local authorities specific powers to spend money on arts and entertainments, thus removing the need to justify activities by linking them closely with books or to disguise them by forming societies. In fairness to local authorities it must be said that many had developed substantial arts programmes through sponsorship of an arts council, such as that in St Pancras which ran a considerable arts festival, whilst other councils (eg Manchester, Dudley and Swindon) had been keen enough to secure the necessary powers by local Acts of Parliament.

Progress after 1948 was at first painfully slow. The pioneers expanded their programmes but many librarians continued to do nothing, often because the post-war economic problems and the rapidly increasing demands for books and information left little time or money beyond the basic services. Nevertheless, the views of the librarian himself again seem to be important in deciding what was done because men continued to carry their ideas from one place to another. James Swift, for instance, having taken part in extension activities at Swindon, became librarian of Holborn and introduced gramophone record recitals, picture exhibitions and other events, although at first the buildings and facilities available were not encouraging. It is possible that the Holborn Council deliberately recruited a librarian with experience in the arts because they wanted the development of the service. This has certainly happened in towns which have established an arts programme and want to continue it.

For many librarians the 1948 Act caused a crisis of conscience. Even the traditional 'extension' work had been, as I have shown, regarded with different degrees of enthusiasm but it was at least nominally designed to encourage book use. The new powers were quite different. Cultural programmes were now to need no special justification but were to be regarded as worthwhile in their own right. This really brought the conflict into the open and librarians could (and did) say that these things are not librarianship. I suspect that some condemned the new powers, even if someone else exercised them, as unfair competition. Every moment spent at a concert or a film show was a moment which could have been better spent reading a book. More commonly, the discussion was at a more sensible level: if a local authority wants to support the arts, is the librarian the appropriate chief officer to act for them?

For some librarians a library should be a cultural centre whose primary function is to render a book service but whose activities extend to all the other media. For others, the library is the part of a cultural centre which is concerned with books. The way in which this difference will be resolved is not yet certain but, in the United Kingdom, the Libraries and Arts Branch of the Department of Education and Science seems, by its title, to express governmental approval for a close link. There is no consistent guidance to be found in other countries for some have made one choice and some another. Even in Scandinavia, where great developments have taken place in both libraries and the arts, one finds the Norwegians favouring the cultural centre which includes a library whilst for the Danes the library is itself the centre.

Nevertheless, there have been many developments since the 1948 Act and within the last few years the pace has quickened. Arts organisations became aware of the powers given to local authorities and began to press their claims for support. Many councils referred their powers to the libraries committee and the chief librarian was the officer required to report and advise. Thus, whether they liked it or not, many librarians found themselves involved with the arts. Most have welcomed the opportunities which have continued to grow as one has to meet the officers of arts organisations in need of help and these contacts lead to others. Increasing sympathy with the claims of artists and musicians has encouraged librarians and their committees to provide more facilities in their buildings and recently built libraries are equipped with exhibition areas, library halls, meeting rooms, and sometimes even full-scale theatres. Within the last year or two it has become apparent that the major events at the central library do not always attract people from the outlying areas and there is increasing pressure to make some space available in branch libraries as well.

Librarians are much more involved in the branch library or neighbourhood activities. The music and record librarian can arrange recitals at the branches and move into the community with events at the old people's luncheon club or at the tenants' associations. Children's librarians may be the contact for entertainments in nursery schools or play centres. All the contacts give opportunities for a link with the library and books need not be forgotten, even when so much is being done that a separate arts section, staffed with its own experts who are not librarians, is formed. This has happened in many of the larger library systems and the main libraries have much more than books to offer.

Already there are libraries which are entered through a foyer which is an exhibition hall. The box office is on one side and signs direct the visitor to the theatre, coffee bar, reference library and the music library. Records may be borrowed or listened to on the premises. At certain times of the day there are story hours for children, lunch-time concerts for adults and evening lectures; there are soft lounge seats for those who would browse through the newspapers, there is a television set and, shortly, there will be videotapes for those who missed a programme or want a repeat performance. Few libraries have all these facilities but very many have a number of them and more and more new buildings will provide them all.

When arts and libraries achieve this kind of balance it is usual to find the controlling committee called the 'libraries and arts' committee and the chief librarian has one of the titles mentioned earlier, eg director of libraries and arts. The other members of the staff are often involved in the community contacts but have less to do with the professionally planned events in theatres, concert halls and exhibition areas. All the librarians need to know what is being offered and can help greatly by encouraging readers, especially at branch libraries, to take part. This is especially important when a town runs an arts festival, which was once the main method of establishing an arts programme in a town. Once the latter has been achieved the importance of festivals should give way to the work of establishing a continual arts programme throughout the year and encouraging regular community work and amateur participation.

Festivals represent such a major effort even for a large libraries and arts department that almost everyone is involved. In my own library system all the branches accept bookings for festival events to help cast the net widely. All the staff are invited to help at events by selling programmes at the door or acting as ushers. They are paid extra for this work and also, of course, have a free viewing of the show. For most of them I think the festival is a highlight of the year, they enjoy the prestige that comes to the department by a successful series of events and they enjoy the general air of excitement.

For the senior staff, even where there is a full-time arts staff, the planning of a festival brings a lot of work. It is a great help if the committee co-opt experts or at least people who are well known for their interest in theatre, music or the visual arts. The librarian, advised by his arts section, can then give the basic facts and administrative details and leave the experts to evaluate the artistic merit of any proposals being considered. Sometimes the co-opted experts can be a little difficult if a festival is planned by the arts sub-committee because each will want to ensure that his particular art form has its fair share of the budget. The elected members hold the balance of voting power but, in practice, the meetings tend to be informal and a librarian with a good knowledge of the locality and a range of contacts with local groups can make a useful contribution.

GRAMOPHONE RECORDS AND PICTURES

Librarians who feel that arranging concerts is not a part of librarianship cannot find the same philosophical objections to sound recordings, pictures and other forms of recording human thoughts and experience. All these things have to be acquired, stored, catalogued and used in much the same way as books. Gramophone records were the first to be accepted as an addition to the basic book service but there were practical difficulties in the early days because the standard (78 rpm) records were brittle and easily damaged. In spite of this the educational use of records was developed as early as 1914 by St Paul's Library, Minnesota, but loans were made only to schools and clubs. The first service to the general public was opened in 1946 at the Chingford branch of the Essex County Library. Again the personal view of the librarian seems to be an important factor because the branch librarian who pioneered the service at Chingford was appointed borough librarian of Walthamstow soon afterwards and he inaugurated a service there in 1947. In the same year record libraries were added at Hampstead, Sutton Coldfield and one or two other places.

Modern discs are much more durable than those available in 1947 and the provision of a service is rapidly being taken for granted. Usually librarians bring together the stock of records and music scores and appoint a specialist to take charge of the complete department. There is still some hesitation about adding records at branch libraries so one must assume that there are librarians who regard them as a special supplementary service rather than part of their basic work.

The range of material in the current catalogues is very wide and many libraries now provide jazz, speech and sound effects, as well as classical records, and a few are beginning to stock at least the best known 'pop music' groups. Language instruction records are the most difficult for the librarian to deal with because the borrower needs to have a complete course for several months or else each disc must be supplied in the right sequence, which means careful organisation of returns and issues if a number of users are working their way through the same set.

Music librarians have had to face many changes, from standard-play records to long-play, from mono to stereo, from stereo to quadraphonic. Discs are being challenged by tapes, cassettes and cartridges. Because the music and record librarians have usually acquired some technical knowledge they seem to be the natural choice for a yet further development of library services with the addition of slides, film strips and videotapes. Any young librarian welcomes at least some experience in this department as the knowledge is also useful later in reference libraries with their microfilm newspapers, photocopying services and other technical aids. Experience with audio-visual equipment is becoming essential for librarians in schools, colleges and universities.

Another extension of library service into the arts field is the loan of pictures. This began later than gramophone record collections and was probably inspired by the availability of good-quality reproductions of major paintings. Framed copies are not of much greater intrinsic value than many of the books in lending libraries and they are not difficult to store. The only problem separating pictures from the normal lending routines is the length of loan period required, books usually being lent for two or three weeks and pictures for three months. The librarians who started collecting reproductions for loan were obviously those who were interested in the visual arts and they mostly chose the works themselves. No great skill is needed as only the outstanding works are reproduced by commercial firms and the reaction of borrowers and the popularity of different styles can give some guidance for future purchases.

A more rewarding policy is to acquire original paintings. Works in local art exhibitions are sometimes of good quality artistically but not unduly expensive and occasionally the head of an art school will act as purchaser. If he buys from ex-students who are beginning to be known the advantages are two-fold: a bargain (as a rule) for the library, and a market and regular exhibition of his work for the artist. A few libraries are now experimenting with lending small items of sculpture and here the obvious way is to start with small multiples which are works repeated a limited number of times and therefore cheaper than unique items.

Every year some enterprising librarian introduces a new extension of his service; sometimes simple and inexpensive schemes are provided like Gravesend's collection of jig-saw puzzles for mentally handicapped children. It would be a good idea to offer this service to all children because no one wants to reassemble the same picture over and over again. Whether this is an extension of the library or of the arts work I do not know. The loan of sound recordings is probably nearer to the library aspect, while the loan of pictures is nearer to the arts, but does it really matter? The great thing is that some librarians are seizing every opportunity to add materials and services which enrich the lives of their patrons.

At a conference on libraries and the arts, Lord Goodman,

then chairman of the Arts Council, put forward a useful philosophy for hesitant librarians:

> Many of us believe that this situation today is not unlike that which existed during the last century over the question of literacy. Then ten per cent of the population were literate and many took the view that this was the proportion determined by the Almighty. Some took a contrary view, and we here today clearly take a contrary view in relation to the arts. I do not believe that the percentage of people who can enjoy great music or enjoy seeing great pictures or reading great literature has been ordained by the Almighty as the same percentage as is enjoying them at this moment. It is a percentage which can be greatly increased to the increase of our happiness.

CHAPTER SEVEN

University and Special Libraries

Public libraries were the only kind I thought about when I started in librarianship. There were comparatively few other opportunities available at that time and I knew very little about those that did exist. Today, the recruit has a very wide field to choose from. Expansion of universities, polytechnics and other forms of higher education has meant setting up many more libraries; even the Open University employs librarians. There are many libraries in institutes, societies, research associations, government departments and in private commercial and industrial firms. Opportunities for librarians have increased not only because there are so many more libraries but also because most of them are now in the care of trained staff. The value of professional education has been accepted and few governing bodies would hand over their libraries, as they once did, to superannuated scholars who know their subjects but are completely ignorant of classification, cataloguing and the techniques of information retrieval.

Thus it is no longer wise to assume that 'librarian' necessarily means 'public librarian'; approximately half the newly qualified now go elsewhere, even if they have had some part of their initial training in public libraries. The attraction of the 'non-public' libraries cannot be summed up in a few simple comparisons because there are so many groups to be considered. The membership of Aslib (Association of Special Libraries and Information Bureaux) includes about 700 libraries maintained by commerce and industry, 120 in government departments and some 160 in institutes of various kinds. Most of the special-subject libraries are very small and lots of them have just one librarian with, perhaps, clerical assistance. Some, however, have staffs of forty or fifty and compare in size with a central public library. Libraries in the field of education are just as varied: there are special libraries in colleges and general libraries in schools and universities. Those in schools and colleges are small and often have only one member of staff whilst those in universities are all substantial and some are very large indeed—staffs varying between fifty or so for some of the newer institutions and several hundred in the great traditional ones.

There are many ways one could group these libraries. The distinction between general and special-subject libraries is important for some purposes as is the difference between the privately owned ones and those in public control, but I doubt whether these logical distinctions tell us nearly as much about the life and work of the librarians concerned as a simple division by size. Librarians who work more or less single-handed have a very different experience from those collaborating with a number of colleagues. The former has an unusually complete view of librarianship, even if the subject area is limited, because he chooses the material, orders, classifies and catalogues it, puts it on the shelves and does everything else that has to be done with it until eventually deciding to throw it away. A large organisation inevitably develops a team approach which almost always leads to a separation of work by function, some of the staff becoming cataloguers, some dealing with service to readers with a possible further subdivision into reference and lending work. A very few large general libraries have tried to avoid this: they divide duties by subject and operate like a group of special libraries under one roof.

School libraries are exceptional because, although the librarian works single-handed, there is often a central organisation co-ordinating all work with schools throughout the area of the education authority. This helps to reduce the routine work as ordering and cataloguing processes can be centralised but the librarian on the spot remains entirely responsible for the service to teachers and children. Naturally I tend to compare and contrast other libraries with the public library service which is within my experience and it seems to me that the school library and the children's department of a public library have a lot in common when they are dealing with school classes or trying to cope with the sudden demand for lots of books on one subject for a school project. A school librarian, however, has a captive audience so that there is less need to attract children to the library although they must still be welcomed and encouraged to read. Story hours are less likely to be called for but instruction in the use of catalogues, indexes and the techniques of obtaining what one wants from a library are all worthwhile. Library lessons are popular with children and many school librarians are highly regarded by both pupils and staff. The disadvantage of the job is the isolation from other librarians and the possibility of being a kind of odd man out in a staff-room otherwise used only by teachers. One needs to work under a headmaster who wants a school library and a librarian to look after it; sometimes there are teachers who will not accept the benefits of library training because they think a library could perfectly well be run by a teacher.

Librarians who want to work with children but for some domestic reason cannot cope with the shift work, including

Saturday work, in a public library really have only the one further option of a school library. Those who simply prefer working in a small organisation with adults have, as I have indicated, a very wide choice. My first close acquaintance with a special library was with the library at Cecil Sharp House, the headquarters of the English Folk Dance and Song Society. The building was to be reconstructed because of damage sustained during the war and this meant moving the library stock. My library had been asked whether we could store the material and perhaps maintain some kind of service, so I went to Cecil Sharp House to find out how many books had to be transported and to see if there were any valuable items needing special care.

On arrival, I found that material was being prepared for a travelling exhibition, including some beautifully made dolls in the national dress of a central European country. The librarian, Margaret Dean Smith, told me about the significance of the various parts of the costume and then showed me the resources of the library for answering questions on such subjects. There were only a few thousand books, mostly on British folk dance and song, but they included a fine set of seventeenth- and eighteenth-century volumes. Valuable items included manuscripts of early folk song and dance collectors, people who trudged around remote villages writing down the legends and songs they found and describing the dances. It was a surprise to find so many periodicals, about eighty I think, worth taking because of their relevance to dance and song. It no longer seemed surprising that so much care and scholarship should be put into this special branch of knowledge or that the librarian should meticulously record and index every detail. 'The librarian', be it noted, not 'one of the librarians'.

One thing I learnt which I have since found at many other small, specialised libraries. The staff have a kind of positive attitude towards information because they serve a limited number of people. They know what the users need, not only in terms of books but also in regard to current information for which they rely on periodicals, photographs, pamphlets, press cuttings and so on. The more specialised the library the more the librarian has to make his own indexes and abstracts. He then does so much more than wait for readers to come to the library: he disseminates information, drawing attention to developments, preparing digests for groups of readers or marking a periodical article for a user with a special interest. Where the various libraries differ is in the pace of their work. The librarian of a daily newspaper has to work fast and at short notice, digging out previous references to a story or to some half-remembered parallel event in the past and ready at any time to offer notes and a photograph for an obituary. Libraries in commerce and industry also have periods of great pressure alternating with less busy spells, whilst those in institutes and learned societies are scholarly and quiet in atmosphere, dealing with a high proportion of their inquiries by post.

A serious disadvantage of many small libraries is that they are housed in *ad hoc* accommodation forming part of a larger building. A public library is usually a separate unit and a librarian works with the architect from the beginning, so that if the resulting structure is unsuitable the librarian is as much to blame as anyone. A society, firm or college has conflicting needs for space and the library is just one of many departments to be included and may not necessarily have the highest priority. Sometimes there are good reasons for any inadequacies but occasionally the firm or institution just goes ahead and builds what the architect thinks will be a good library. One of the worst examples I have seen was the newly opened library of a college of education. It had ample space, was well furnished and had a good stock of books and magazines. All this was ruined by a split level design which looked good but involved having two exits, both out of sight of the staff desk. Did the architect expect lecturers and teachers-in-training to be beyond reproach? No practising librarian would trust an archbishop not to walk off (absent-mindedly, of course) with a book or article needed for a sermon.

One of the sad things learnt by the special librarian is that experts do not show the great reverence for the important materials of their speciality that one might hope. I knew a case where a musician ruined a fine set of the complete works of J. S. Bach by ripping out a score which took up the centre section of one volume, all because a separate version of the score was not immediately available. Scholars cannot always be trusted to handle rare works without supervision and I have known several cases in which a hard-to-come-by item has been lent as a special privilege only to be subsequently reported as having been lost. After receiving a bill for the replacement cost, estimated about fifty per cent above the real value, the borrower usually finds the item was merely mislaid and returns it. Law students surely should have special respect for the rules but law books disappear faster than most; even textbooks on larceny are stolen.

These things about the users can be learnt from experience when one has started working in a special library but there has been disagreement about the pre-entry qualifications. Can any librarian run any kind of library or does he need a knowledge of the subject of a special library? For a long time the ineffectiveness of fine libraries run by dilettante scholars led to an over-emphasis on the need for techniques and most librarians have claimed that they could be applied to any subject. This is true, but it is surely better if a librarian has a real interest in the material he handles and wants to keep abreast of developments, reads the reviews of new books and glances at the periodicals. Many of the users of special libraries are knowledgeable in the subject covered and some may be experts. They will be irritated by a new librarian who fails to grasp a technical term or even neglects to have a basic guide to hand so that a term can be placed in the right context. One would expect a librarian who has no interest in music to be in some difficulty if faced with the task of sorting out music scores and parts for rebinding. Ability to read a score, to identify the key and to understand a thematic catalogue is a useful asset for anyone working in a music library, if not an absolute essential.

A few special libraries are open for long hours or are needed on certain evenings but lots of them serve an organisation which needs them during normal office hours only. This is attractive for staff who find difficulty in fitting into the shift systems operated in national, university and public libraries to cover evening and week-end duties. I know several librarians who went into special libraries for just this reason but there are many who choose the work for its own sake. Most special librarians begin their careers in university or public libraries to gain all-round experience and, often, to take advantage of training schemes and secondment to library schools which could not be offered by a small organisation. A few recruits with good academic qualifications intend to make a career in public libraries but transfer because they feel that their abilities are not being fully used. This can be just a matter of luck, because a trainee returning from a library school cannot expect that there will be an automatic vacancy in the department which is his first choice and, if there is no prospect of a transfer within a year or so, it may be wiser to get out rather than spend years on less congenial work.

Special libraries offer a vast range of subjects and there is even a choice of libraries in the same subject area of interest. Few of us would be equally happy in every possible subject but there is sometimes a surprisingly wide choice of jobs in even very narrow fields. For instance, there are enough libraries limited to biology for Aslib to have a special Biological Group where members can meet to discuss common problems. There are also Aeronautical, Economics, Social Sciences and Textiles Groups, although the libraries concerned vary in size from the one-man (or woman) organisation I have mentioned to considerable collections with large staffs.

Most of the larger libraries are supported by public funds, although they are not public libraries in the usual sense. There is a library at the House of Commons to provide members of parliament with background facts and up-to-date information; each department of state has a library and various public corporations such as the British Broadcasting Corporation and the Central Electricity Generating Board have libraries. All of these provide secure employment and offer contracts broadly similar to those in local government. Some of them are library systems with branch establishments serving regional office or research units away from the headquarters. The BBC is among this group but it must be unique in its range of library use: production information for radio justified a large reference library but television brought fresh needs in costuming, decor and all sorts of facts to avoid howlers such as anachronisms in plays, so that an additional reference library was established. There is also an External Services library and the Monitoring Unit library, both supervised by the central reference librarian. Music is such a large commitment in broadcasting that a separate music library was set up with perhaps the largest sound recordings collection in the world. Sound and now video records of the BBC's own broadcasts are an ever-growing archive which must be stored so that subjects and specific items can be found when needed. Apart from all this there is the need to stock material on the technical aspects of broadcasting.

Government departments do not have libraries quite on

this scale but various ministries have been reorganised and enlarged in scope. The Department of Trade and Industry, for instance, was formed from the Board of Trade and the Ministry of Technology which was itself an amalgamation of parts of other units. Before the fourteen libraries in the DTI could be fully brought into a central administration, the government again changed the structure, including the removal of responsibility for supply of energy which became a separate ministry. Librarians in the government service have the main burden of coping with these changes but every kind of library has the job of cross-indexing all the material relating to government. Public reference libraries, for instance, have strong collections on local government affairs to provide information for councillors and these include many departmental hand-outs. At one time there was a separate board for local government affairs and then, for many years, the Department of Health incorporated this section. By the time all the catalogues in the country had settled down under 'Health' a new government set up a Ministry of Housing and then made it Housing and Local Government. Periodical publications and those forming part of a series needed complicated cross-referencing if readers were to trace them through the various issuing departments and by the time everything was tidy again local government affairs became part of the Department of the Environment. I wonder if any prime minister ever thinks of the hidden costs of his latest reorganisation.

None of the librarians in government service or the public corporations has the kind of autonomy enjoyed by the public librarian who is a chief officer in a local authority. The library is very important to some departments and the librarian reports to a very senior civil servant but he is still responsible to such an officer. Elsewhere the status is lower because the influence on line management is less important. A friend of mine who went into a government library found lots of civil servants who were senior to him insisting on their own copies of various magazines, all ordered through the library, although one or two copies circulated quickly would have been adequate. He also found the cream of the library's current directories scattered through the department as each administrator liked to have his own 'window ledge' library. The new librarian protested about the extravagance of all this on every suitable and unsuitable occasion until his constantly reiterated views somehow reached the ears of an under-secretary. A report was called for and rapidly approved. A directive gave the librarian the authority he needed to do his job properly.

UNIVERSITY LIBRARIES

Every librarian has to develop ways of dealing with users who expect special privileges. University librarians have the most difficult problem because they have to reconcile the dual function of the university, catering for research as well as education. Undergraduates are numerous enough to occupy all the space in reference departments and to make lending libraries at times seem as busy as a public library. Teaching staff then want books at short notice, or they want a book for a long time. They order books as a matter of urgency but then never borrow them. Some professors want the library to emphasise their own subjects even if everything else has to be neglected. How does one argue with a professor who is the world authority and himself wrote the most important works on a subject he is pressing on the librarian? Delaying tactics are perhaps the only ones that work.

The importance of the research aspect varies a lot between one university and another. I do not want to lose too many friends among university librarians but I must say that I find many of the newer libraries not altogether unlike the large city public libraries. They do not, of course, receive requests for 'two romances and a blood for dad' and they do not have to cope with small children. On the other hand, as I love to tell my colleagues, a far higher proportion of the general public using my library are graduates than the university librarians realise; the more the universities expand, the more undergraduates they have to serve and, a few years later, the more graduates there are using public libraries. However, there are only a few public libraries which have special collections of research material presented in the past or built up to meet special needs but most of the older universities have impressive source material which any librarian must view with respect. Preserving these collections is a great responsibility and the librarians sometimes become authorities on the subjects they care for. For a very long time this aspect so dominated their work that administration and control of library processes seemed to be curiously antiquated but, in the last ten years or so, there has been a quiet revolution. To some extent this has been forced on the university librarians because the post-war expansion brought new pressures and the kind of mass use which public librarians had known for years.

Between 1966 and 1970 many British university librarians had to cope with increases of sixty or seventy per cent in the number of book loans they dealt with and some doubled their use of the inter-library lending network, giving an overall growth rate nearly twice as large as that of the public library system during the same period. Routine processes had to be adapted quickly and university librarians began to take much more interest in what was happening in the more advanced public libraries. The traditional pattern of organisation with sub-librarians in charge of lending, reading-rooms, and so on is changing in some places to a subject division of work which limits the number of people served by each librarian and so helps to retain the more personal service which was in danger of being lost. Developments of the last ten years or so have involved the library staff more closely in the teaching function of the university and, in some places, librarians have developed the use of recordings, language laboratories, film and other visual aids.

In America the growth of the university special collections since the war has been remarkable, especially in source material such as serials, documents and government publications. Very many American universities now number their library stocks in millions and the rate of growth is increasing all the time. The emphasis on the research aspect probably accounts for the wider gaps between American university and public librarians than one finds in Britain where a common interest in techniques has multiplied contacts, at least between the senior staff. British libraries growing on a scale in any way comparable to those in America are mainly the ones which can obtain free copies of British publications under the copyright Acts: the Bodleian (Oxford), Cambridge university library and the library at Trinity College, Dublin.

The day-to-day work of a university librarian has many things in common with the duties of a public librarian but there is more specialisation and few university librarians meet the variety of subjects covered in a public reference library. Also, of course, they miss the more trivial inquiries and there is a special satisfaction in dealing with work in greater depth or in some abstruse subjects. The atmosphere of a university is congenial to many; anyone who has chosen to work with books and information is bound to have some feeling for an academic world, although there are still problems. The school projects, for instance, which sometimes plague the public library staff are simpler preliminaries to the later advanced work of writing a thesis. The basic problem for the librarian is just the same: to give guidance that is needed in bibliographical matters and to provide the material but to avoid becoming involved to the point where the student or researcher is deprived of the experience of doing his own work.

THE NATIONAL LIBRARIES

The three university libraries mentioned above have some of the characteristics of national libraries, the Bodleian and Cambridge university libraries because of their size and Trinity College because it is the only library in Eire with the privilege of copyright deposit. The Bodleian, with over 3 million books and 50,000 manuscripts, is one of the oldest and most important libraries in the world. Its modern extension is an interesting addition to the main seventeenth-century building and seems to epitomise the problems faced by the staff in bringing the organisation up to date; one meets keen librarians applying computer techniques to the vagaries of early catalogues and providing a service that is far from antiquated. I think it is a good place to work. The library of Trinity College, Dublin, is smaller, having about a million volumes looked after by a non-manual staff of 58 (Bodley has 300). Trinity boasts a new building, opened in the late 1960s, which has been skilfully designed to harmonise with the Palladian edifice adjoining it whilst inside it is almost aggressively modern. Although the service is mainly used by the university, the library holds many national treasures, including the unique *Book of Kells* and other ancient manuscripts.

Scotland and Wales have specifically national libraries. The Scottish National Library, in Edinburgh, was founded in 1682 and now has nearly 3 million books and a large collection of manuscripts of Scottish interest. The National Library of Wales stands magnificently on a hill just outside Aberystwyth. It is a later foundation but has been a copyright library since 1911 and now has about 2 million books, including many special collections relating to Wales and other Celtic countries. It also has some fine topographical prints, drawings by Thomas Rowlandson and etchings by Augustus John; all of which sounds like a local history librarian's dreams come true on a grand scale.

The greatest library of all for research work is the one known to generations of librarians as the BML (British Museum Library), now officially the Reference Division of the British Library. Theoretically the library is a public one because it is financed from taxation and admission is not restricted to the members of a particular group, but readers' tickets are issued only to those whose needs cannot be met through the local library service. Whenever there is a news item about the British Museum library someone mentions that Karl Marx did a lot of work there and the effects of his *Das Kapital* have been so vast that it provides the perfect opening for a few lines about the pen being mightier than the sword. Many other writers and thinkers have also used the national library and one is tempted to say that it is a place where people go to write books rather than to read them. A survey carried out by a government committee found that over half the users were carrying out research which would take them many months to complete.

Clearly the kind of people to be encountered at the library come from a limited section of the population. The librarians are not bothered by the mass of people who use public libraries, by trivial requests or by professors who regard themselves as having a proprietorial right. They have more than their share of eccentrics but most of their users are genuinely involved in scholarship and original thinking. The subject range is wide but slanted towards the humanities rather than the sciences (at the main library, that is). Much of the work of the staff is similar to the tasks needed in smaller establishments and when I meet staff from the BML I am always a little surprised to find how many problems we have in common. Sir Frank Francis, director and principal librarian until a few years ago, was concerned with plans for a new building which would be about ten times as big as the largest public library while I was concerned with plans much less grandiose but we both had the same problems about getting plans approved and then persuading a committee to vote the money. Discussions about library use of computers also seem to involve a lot of common ground: few public libraries have to worry about the optical scanning of non-Roman alphabets but they share with national and university libraries the complexities of filing order and the costing difficulties of converting existing catalogues.

Considered on their merits as working establishments the great national libraries of the world are impressive by their vast stocks and by the statistics quoted about them. The British Museum library has over 8 million books occupying more than 150 miles of shelving and the Library of Congress has 16 million books and pamphlets filling over 270 miles of shelves. Direct comparison is not valid as the libraries are not constituted in quite the same way. The Library of Congress, besides acting as the national library, is also the library of a legislature and is therefore, in British terms, incorporating the library of the House of Commons as well. It also carries out a number of other functions which, in Britain, have been dealt with by separate organisations only now being brought together as parts of the British Library.

The university or public librarian who has not studied the matter in detail is at first inclined to think of the labours involved in running the smaller libraries that he knows and to wonder how even an army of librarians could cope with these millions of books. To get a proper perspective on national libraries we must consider one more statistic which is less often quoted: the amount of use that is made of the stored material. Book use at the British Museum is roughly equivalent to some 10 per cent of the total stock being required each year and, as in most of these vast libraries, the majority of the books do nothing for years on end except occupy the miles of shelving so often quoted. This is not a criticism, for an important part of the duty of a national library is to preserve literature for posterity, current use being limited to meeting needs which cannot easily be satisfied elsewhere. From the point of view of the staff the relationship between total stock, book use and annual intake is important because it governs the nature of the work they have to do.

The average use of books in public libraries is equal to every book being borrowed six times a year. This average is brought down by the large reserve of stocks at headquarters' libraries, which may rarely be used, and this low level of use is offset by the intensive use of stock at branch libraries, where each book is used eight or more times a year. The work of acquiring and cataloguing a book has to be done only once so that, for public librarians, book processing is a small part of their duties when compared with the labour of lending a book over and over again, receiving it back, replacing it on the shelves and completing the other routines of book use. In the British Museum library much of the stock gives no further trouble once it has reached the shelves and so, proportionately, the initial acquisition processes are a much more important part of the work.

The national library is so large and has such a complex organisation that no generalisations can be made about the work of the staff. There is a broad framework which suggests a functional division of duties (cataloguing and service aspects) but there are special subject sections as well. These deal with state papers, rare books, newspapers, music and philately, subjects which thus bypass the main catalogue section. Certain languages (Slavonic, East European) are dealt with separately within the general department, their own experts doing selection, acquisition and cataloguing.

Western material is divided into departments for printed books and for manuscripts whilst the oriental department includes both forms of record. This is all very complex and obviously scholars, librarians and scholar-librarians are all needed.

The incorporation of the British Museum library in the British Library is likely to expand the services it renders to other libraries. It has always been important for reasons other than direct services to readers as it has provided immense catalogues which are used daily in the bibliographical services of most other libraries of any standing. It has very efficient photocopying facilities and can supply microfilm versions of quite obscure newspapers and other periodicals. The massive building in Bloomsbury is awesome to most of us because of its history of hospitality to scholars and thinkers but we reserve the right to complain of the inadequate opening hours, long delays in finding books and the lack of national co-ordinating services. It will take a long time for the changes to begin to notice but the library is now started on a path which the unkind would say will drag it kicking and screaming into the twentieth century. Alas, it will also take a long time before the desperately needed new building is in use.

> I remember the days when the Superintendent of the North Library at the British Museum spent his morning writing letters in Latin to a fellow librarian at the Bibliothèque Nationale in Paris. A good lunch followed and an afternoon spent in slumber. Those days seem far off indeed . . . (Nick Childs, librarian of Brunel University, writing in *The Times Higher Education Supplement*.)

CHAPTER EIGHT

Training and Prospects

The Library Association has existed for nearly a hundred years to promote the interests of libraries and of librarians. Other national organisations include a geographical limitation in their titles, eg the American Library Association, and I used to think that the British librarians of 1877 were a shade arrogant in assuming that theirs was 'the' association. If they had been the first in the field there might be some excuse but the American body, founded in 1876, had that honour. I later found that the original intention had been to form 'The Library Association of the United Kingdom', a more modest title but one which was bound to get abbreviated. The Royal Charter which incorporated the association in 1898 refers throughout to The Library Association.

There are now similar organisations in many parts of the world and the International Federation of Library Associations is a flourishing body whose council, meeting in Liverpool in 1971, attracted 750 delegates from more than sixty countries. Objectives of most of the groups include promoting libraries and librarianship, supporting legislation and encouraging research. A few associations include the working conditions in libraries and the welfare of librarians in their general responsibilities and almost all are concerned with the education of librarians. An important difference between British and American practice has been the system of training, certification and registration. In the United States, education is the responsibility of graduate library schools which award degrees in library science, the American Library Association merely approving curricula and giving recognition to schools where appropriate. This pattern has been reproduced in the many countries which looked to America when they set up their library systems.

The British practice is more complicated as it offers several ways of entering the profession. The first formal training was arranged by the Library Association which had a clear duty set out in the Royal Charter: 'To promote whatever may tend to the improvement of the position and qualifications of librarians', and 'To hold examinations in librarianship and to issue certificates of efficiency'. The Association has carried out this task from the beginning but for a long time it had little influence on the methods by which students prepared for the examinations. Provided one complied with the required educational standards based on the General Certificate of Education an application to sit the examinations was accepted. In the past, many entrants studied by correspondence courses, evening classes or other part-time schooling, meantime earning their living as library assistants. At one time almost all the routine counter work and book shelving in libraries was done by such staff and every recruit for any job (except uniformed attendants) was regarded as a librarian in training.

This apprenticeship system had many advantages. For the assistant the great benefit was a continuous contact with books and readers which is the basis of all librarianship. For the library there was a certainty that all the staff had a fairly high level of general education and a proportion of them would be partly trained. The bad side of the system was the need for people who had done a full day's work to sit down and study when they ought to have had an opportunity for recreation. Many took years and years to qualify and had little social life outside their work. After the war a system of full-time education for librarianship developed fairly rapidly and the examination syllabuses gradually changed so that part-time preparation was discouraged.

The Association's examinations are at present divided into two groups to allow for both graduate and non-graduate recruitment but there is some talk of aiming at an all-graduate profession. Non-graduates must expect to spend two years in full-time study at a school of librarianship to prepare for the general professional examinations which are in two parts. Part 1 consists of four papers which must be taken at one and the same sitting, thus discouraging part-time study which could scarcely prepare one for more than two papers at a time. Subjects are: the library and the community, government and control of libraries, organisation of knowledge, bibliographical control and service. Part 2 of the examinations consists of six papers which may be taken in any order from groups offering a fair amount of choice. One paper is chosen from List A giving options between public, academic and special libraries and others are taken from List B which allows for specialisation in classification, cataloguing, work with children or other departmental groups. List C deals with the bibliography and librarianship of special subjects and candidates can choose from a wide range such as 'English literature from 1750' or 'Literature for children', with the alternative of a specific subject such as music, medicine, education and so on.

The minimum pre-entry qualifications include a General Certificate of Education in five subjects, of which one must be English language and two must be at Advanced level. Most of the schools of librarianship prefer students to have a year's experience in a library before undertaking a course but a few accept entrants straight from school and then run a seven-term course which includes a full term's attachment to a library for practical work. For most people the timetable is likely to be: one year's paid work as a trainee immediately after taking 'A' levels at school, two academic years at library school and, finally, one more year working as a pre-professional at a higher salary level to complete the requirements for registration as a chartered librarian.

The examinations for post-graduate students require one year's full-time study. They consist of five compulsory and two optional subjects covering similar ground to those outlined. Two of the subjects are course-assessed instead of being tested by written examinations and, by agreeing to this, the Library Association for the first time relaxed its rigid control over examinations. Since then the Association has been moving slowly nearer to the American practice of approving a course and the general pattern of training and then allowing the school or college to arrange its own internal examinations. Diplomas from approved courses give complete exemption from the Association's own examinations. A further development has been the degree courses in librarianship which are now available both at universities and at some polytechnics, the latter being under the auspices of the Council for National Academic Awards. Even this is not the end of the options for there is a choice between a general degree in librarianship taking three years and an honours degree taking four years. Exactly what status these degrees achieve in relation to a non-vocational degree followed by post-graduate training in librarianship remains to be seen but combining academic and vocational studies is in line with some other professions in the United Kingdom and with the practice of librarianship in some other countries.

The Association publishes a leaflet, *How to Become a Chartered Librarian*, and also issues an annual *Students' Handbook* which gives full details of the educational qualifications required, the courses of study available and the regulations governing registration. Potential students will find it worthwhile to contact their local public library or their school or college library to discuss the application of the rules to their own particular circumstances. There are so many choices to be made, beginning with the option to aim at a degree or settle for the two-year non-graduate course which requires much the same preliminary certificates.

Local newspapers occasionally give information about vacancies in the various departments of the borough or county council but offers are also made known to youth employment officers, careers masters or university appointments boards. Failing any of these there is no possible harm in writing direct to the chief librarian of a local library asking whether he or his staff officer could advise on a career in librarianship. The best openings to seek are those which are formal training schemes run by an authority to ensure that its future needs for trained staff are met. A recognised trainee is given favourable terms for practical training, secondment to library school on full or part salary and a guaranteed job on return.

I would not advise anyone to proceed direct to a school of librarianship from their sixth form or from university but anyone who really wants to do this should write to several schools because there are always more applicants for librarianship courses than there are places. The disadvantages of direct entry is that no one can be quite sure he has chosen the right job if he has not tried it; very few trainees do change their minds during their first year's work but there is no shame in doing so and no time or money has been wasted on abortive training. The choice of papers and the course based on them is made much easier for those who have had enough experience to know which kind of work they prefer. At the very least a year in a library should suffice to tell a recruit the departments he does *not* want as a long-term ambition. A large library system will have former trainees whose uncensored comments about library schools add a lot to the official statements in brochures.

Annual wage and salary adjustments have become part of modern life and there is little sign of inflation ending, which means that details of cash rewards may have little meaning by the time they are printed. However, in the early part of 1974 (before the annual claim had been settled) a trainee in local government could expect a starting salary of £1,131 per annum if a non-graduate of 18 or £1,416 if he joined later as a graduate. Chartered librarians, both graduate and non-graduate, could expect a minimum of £1,926 in public libraries. (All the above figures would be higher for those working in the London area and there are additional payments for any hours worked after midday on Saturdays.) University libraries offer starting salaries not very different from those quoted for public libraries but, if a good honours degree is specified, there may be a salary range giving guaranteed progression to £3,000 or more. Almost all librarians have reasonably good conditions of service including holidays, sickness pay arrangements and pensions schemes. Senior posts in public, university and a few industrial libraries carry salaries of over £6,000 to more than £7,000 per annum. In local government some employers offer travelling and other expense allowances which are very necessary in the large library systems now in existence. Librarians appointed directors of leisure or of libraries and arts may receive much higher salaries than quoted, the salary being related to the size of the population served.

Thoughtful recruits will want to consider the likely developments in librarianship as well as the financial rewards. How far will the young man or woman coming into the profession today find the story given in the earlier chapters of this book still relevant? How far are libraries likely to change during the remainder of the twentieth century? No one would dare to be dogmatic but there are some pointers to likely developments. Although libraries have expanded enormously since World War II the growth has barely kept pace with developments in education. A period of consolidation seems likely in universities and possibly in polytechnics but the after effects of what has already been done should ensure library advances for some years to come. Public libraries have always shown increased use following extensions in education and all the previous experience suggests steady growth for some time ahead. All the varied services of public libraries are likely to expand, not only the basic book service, because most economists are predicting increased leisure over the next few decades. This will mean pressure to develop the recreational and cultural aspect of libraries as well as the educational purposes. In short, librarianship is still a 'growth industry' and redundancy or unemployment for chartered librarians is not very likely in the foreseeable future.

Prospects for individual librarians have changed in the past decade because of the mergers and amalgamations of the bodies which control libraries. Reference has been made to the changes in London in 1965 and to those in the rest of England and Wales in 1974; reorganisation of local government in Scotland is due in 1975 but the changes will be less sweeping as far as local authority libraries are concerned. These great reforms occur at very long intervals and a new entrant to local government today is unlikely to see any similar large scale changes during his working life. Restructuring of government departments has also been mentioned and I can only repeat that we seem to have been living through a period when every new government spends more energy remodelling the machinery of administration than it does in using it. This phase may pass soon if only because of the increasingly vocal opposition of the civil servants who suffer the fruitless moves.

Special libraries in industry have not been exempt from

the trend towards ever larger units; combinations, mergers and take-over bids have had much the same effects as the reorganisations of central and local government, with the added problem that some industrial librarians have been made redundant in 'rationalisation' changes. The main difference in every kind of library has been fewer but more responsible top jobs and more senior posts just below that level. The implications for the education and training of librarians seem to be a need to produce more specialists and fewer chief librarians. In the past there has been a tendency to regard every recruit as a potential chief and train him accordingly.

The main administrative changes have been made and the only uncertainty is the long-term effects. Technical changes have been rapid in recent years and are still continuing and likely to continue. Many people are surprised to learn that librarians are already using computers to handle dull routine jobs such as sorting the records of books issued and returned to the library. In large systems many millions of transactions a year have to be dealt with and the sorting and matching of the files is a task very well suited to mechanisation. Some libraries are using computers to handle all the 'business' side of lending library work and all overdue book and recall notices, reservations and other routines are fully mechanised. Most of the work transferred to computers was previously done by clerical and other non-professional staff and there is no likelihood of any very large percentage reduction in total staff. Benefits are sought in improved efficiency and accuracy with a consequent reduction in complaints from readers.

Producing library catalogues by computer is more fruitful in achieving savings in costs and staff time but the benefits depend on the size and complexity of the library system. Again there is very little reduction in professional work, as the librarians are still required to make decisions on the classification and cataloguing information to be fed into the computer so that any savings are in the clerical and non-professional time previously needed for duplicating and sorting catalogue cards. Print-out from the computer is usually direct to sheets which can be photocopied and bound together as a catalogue in book form but recent developments show a move towards computer production of microfilm for all kinds of catalogues and indexes.

Economic pressures are bound to lead to further mechanisation in libraries and the formation of the larger units brings forward the time when any particular process is worth transferring to the computer. During the change-over period there is a lot more work for librarians, especially cataloguers, in liaison with systems analysts and programmers. Many librarians have had to acquire at least a rudimentary understanding of computer operations but none of the chief librarians who have been introducing mechanisation over the past decade or so learnt anything about computers when they were being trained; indeed, it would be perfectly possible to qualify today without hearing very much about data processing. Possibly only a small proportion of tomorrow's librarians will need to know much on this subject. The pioneers of mechanisation had to know just what they were doing but, once the new systems are operating, their day-to-day running will not require much technical knowledge. I suspect, however, that this is another field where technical changes will be frequent.

A further development in routine work during the next decade or so may be the use of the computer to analyse library processes and provide a feed-back of information which can be of assistance in management. Demand for a particular title or for certain subjects could be precisely analysed and orders for extra copies to reduce waiting lists could be made automatically. I have previously mentioned the importance of library siting and this, too, could be computed and 'catchment' areas analysed scientifically. The extent to which the age structure of a population affects library use both in terms of total use and of type of material could also be found accurately and might have practical effects in planning. How far librarians and their controlling committees will want to go in automating services can only be guessed. There will always be a substantial area for the exercise of human initiative and judgement. Computers are much more easily programmed to measure quantity than quality and they are not likely to replace the librarian's value judgements which cause him to put some titles in every library even though he expects usage to be low.

During the 1960s some librarians, especially in America, were experimenting with uses of computers which went far beyond the idea of a machine to improve the efficiency of routine work. Instead of merely recording details of books in the computer's memory-bank they wanted to read in the contents of the books. If the facts and information people require can be stored in such a way that retrieval is almost instantaneous, why have the books at all? At any rate their use could perhaps be reduced. In a very specific subject the idea does not present insuperable problems and maybe future developments in technology will enlarge the areas to which such a technique might be applied. The real question is whether the effort will be worthwhile.

Books are themselves very compact ways of storing facts and they are, if properly indexed, very easily and quickly used to release the information they contain. Problems of providing easy and reliable access to a mass of machine-readable facts plus the delays of having to activate a particular section of the computer's store for each single reference suggest that it will never be worthwhile abandoning the book as a fact and information store except in limited areas. The use of books for most other kinds of reading is not even threatened by the computer, and the computer is a positive hindrance to those who need to browse. Serendipity is the essence of the casual use of libraries.

Librarians being trained today are unlikely to need more than a general knowledge of computer capabilities (unless, of course, the predictions in the previous section prove to be wildly wrong and magnetic tape and disc stores really form the sole contents of the future library). Librarians will, however, certainly need to prepare for a vast expansion of other non-book stores which already exist in some libraries and are increasing rapidly in their importance to library users. Few could fail to be impressed by the enormous space saving made by the pioneering libraries which replaced their bound volumes of *The Times* with 35mm roll film and many libraries followed suit, eventually adding photographic copies of local newspapers as well. Gradually other microforms have crept into use for other purposes and new kinds of reading machines have been developed, some of them including facilities for making immediate prints of any part of the film on request.

Reference library staffs already need to know something about photographic services and to have a good knowledge of the equipment which is available. They also, unfortunately, have to keep pace with the ever-developing jargon and ever-changing groups of initials. COM, unheard of a few years ago, means computer output on microfilm and implies a direct conversion from magnetic tape to film. This is a valuable aid to rapid production of catalogues and bibliographies from the stored information but, before the news of COM had reached the far-flung branches of the service, a further development of it appeared as PCMI (photo chromic micro image). This is a much reduced copy made possible by the skill of chemists in using special film emulsions to give the necessary resolution. PCMI frames are so small that a postcard-size sheet of film carries the complete scores of all Beethoven's symphonies. Half a dozen such cards record the full catalogue entries of a whole year of British book publishing and there is ample space for an index section on one of the cards.

Such developments are spectacular in their implications for compact storage of records and no librarian dare ignore them. Few, however, would venture to look very far into the future to predict the new marvels which scientists will produce and which are relevant to librarianship. Perhaps, in view of the many problems of copyright which must arise from all the photocopying, filming and microfilming, librarians may have less need to peer into the future than have authors and publishers who need to safeguard their products.

'Non-book' material in libraries, other than microforms, has been mentioned in other chapters where is was implied that the development of gramophone record libraries, picture loan schemes, the use of sound and videotape cassettes and the provision of film strips and audio-visual aids generally are all in their infancy. Here one can speak with confidence. Changes have been quite rapid since the first gramophone record collections were started and further changes in the facilities provided by libraries must be expected, even if their exact nature cannot be foreseen. Certainly many more people will want these things and the task of coping with the demands for materials already in use will mean a great change in most libraries.

While all these technical changes have been happening, less publicised changes have affected librarianship in the basic work of supplying books and other printed material. More complex classification and indexing methods have been evolved to cope with the greater output of literature of all kinds. In twenty years after the war the number of titles published annually in the United Kingdom almost doubled but, of course, the increase in each separate year was small and could be coped with by a slight readjustment of the time given to book selection and processing. Over the whole period catalogues and classification systems have become noticeably more complex. Perhaps even more important than the number of book titles is the total output of information in reports, periodicals, abstracts and all the ways in which discoveries and ideas are promulgated. From time to time this too can make headlines about the 'information explosion' but the year-by-year, relentless increase in the amount of material, in its complexity and its more involved relationships with existing knowledge is real enough. Research libraries become more and more vital in an advanced technological civilisation and the need to arrange, classify and retrieve information applies regardless of the means of recording it.

The fundamentals of a librarian's work have not changed very much and are unlikely to change in the near future. Simple definitions which insist that a library is a place in which books are stored need to be amended but libraries do still store them. They have to, because they continue to transmit a cultural heritage from generation to generation as well as serve immediate practical objectives. Perhaps I have managed to show that the dictionary definition of a librarian as the custodian of a library is about as accurate as describing a priest as the custodian of a church.

Appendix 1

INFORMATION ABOUT LIBRARIANSHIP

Inquiries should be addressed to: The Secretary, The Library Association, 7 Ridgmount Street, London, WC1E 7AE. (Pamphlets are issued on *How to Become a Chartered Librarian*, on careers in librarianship for graduates and on work in special libraries.)

SCHOOLS OF LIBRARIANSHIP

University schools exist in the following places: Belfast (Queen's University), Glasgow (University of Strathclyde), London (University College), Loughborough (University of Technology), Sheffield (University of Sheffield).

Non-university schools (some linked with nearby universities or awarding CNAA degrees) are at: Aberdeen, Aberystwyth, Birmingham, Brighton, Leeds, Liverpool, London (Ealing Technical College and also the Polytechnic of North London), Loughborough, Manchester, Newcastle.

APPENDIX 1

APPOINTMENTS

Direct application to the librarian of any library is an acceptable practice.

Vacancies for qualified librarians are advertised in *The Times Literary Supplement, The Times Educational Supplement* and in professional journals.

Posts in special libraries are sometimes notified to: ASLIB, 3 Belgrave Square, London, SW1.

Appendix 2

Table A shows the growth of book lending in a few typical cities since the time of Andrew Carnegie. Table B shows the development of gramophone record loans in a selection of London boroughs since they were enlarged. (1886 means the year ending 31 March 1886 and so on.)

TABLE A ANNUAL BOOK LOANS

	Birmingham	*Leeds*	*Nottingham*	*Sheffield*
1886	478,903	732,465	294,528	399,653
1914	2,217,563	1,382,237	569,146	733,488
1970	9,489,272	5,388,014	2,961,250	4,915,892

TABLE B ANNUAL LOANS OF SOUND RECORDINGS

	Barnet	*Camden*	*Islington*	*Tower Hamlets*
1967	82,579	386,208	42,723	58,491
1968	90,078	523,515	59,104	64,836
1969	86,347	534,622	61,121	64,577
1970	85,908	516,764	60,709	64,384
1971	112,876	530,191	56,742	70,516
1972	126,523	563,688	59,131	73,881

Bibliography

REFERENCE

The Libraries, Museums and Art Galleries Year Book. Gives details of all types of library, including the librarian's name, the stock, special collections, total staff and number qualified. Very useful to those considering applying for jobs.

The Library Association. *Students' Handbook* (annual). Gives the regulations covering professional examinations together with the detailed syllabus and a guide to facilities for study.

Who's Who in Librarianship and Information Science. Gives information about most British librarians, including present and previous posts, publications and interests. Very useful to candidates for jobs who get as far as an interview.

READING

Atkinson, Frank. *Librarianship: An Introduction to the Profession* (Clive Bingley, 1974)

Corbett, E. V. *Introduction to Librarianship* (James Clarke, 2nd ed, 1970)

Dearden, James. *Books Are for People: A Librarian's Life* (Educational Explorers, 1969)

Gerard, David E. (ed). *Libraries and the Arts* (Clive Bingley, 1970)

Kelly, Thomas. *A History of Public Libraries in Great Britain, 1845–1965* (The Library Association, 1973)

Kyle, Barbara R. F. *Teach Yourself Librarianship* (English University Press, 1964)

Murison, W. J. *The Public Library: Its Origins, Purpose and Significance* (Harrap, 2nd ed, 1971)

Thompson, James. *An Introduction to University Library Administration* (Clive Bingley, 1970)

Index